WHAT SIZE
ARE GOD'S SHOES?

Kids, Chaos,
and the
Spiritual Life

WHAT SIZE
ARE GOD'S SHOES?

Kids, Chaos, and the Spiritual Life

Tim Schenck

MOREHOUSE PUBLISHING

Morehouse Publishing
An Imprint of Church Publishing Incorporated
Harrisburg – New York

Morehouse Publishing, 4775 Linglestown Road, Harrisburg, PA 17105

Morehouse Publishing, 445 Fifth Avenue, New York, NY 10016

Morehouse Publishing is an imprint of Church Publishing Incorporated.

Cover art by Charles Hefling

Library of Congress Cataloging-in-Publication Data

Schenck, Timothy.
  What size are God's shoes? : kids, chaos, and the spiritual life / Timothy Schenck.
      p. cm.
  ISBN 978-0-8192-2312-8 (pbk.)
  1. Christian life. I. Title.
  BV4515.3.S3435 2008
  248.4--dc22
                                      2008007409

Printed in the United States of America

08 09 10 11 12 13   10 9 8 7 6 5 4 3 2 1

In memory of my father, Andrew Schenck (1940–1992),
who taught me much about faith and fatherhood

CONTENTS

ACKNOWLEDGMENTS

"Acknowledgments" pages in books are funny things. I'm not sure if anyone actually reads them. Who cares if the author wants to thank the family dog? (No offense, Delilah—and thanks, by the way.) If you've read this far, you're probably searching for your name. I apologize if it doesn't appear. I really wanted to include it, but there was no more space. Sorry. It's the publisher's fault, not mine.

Now that I've weeded out most of the readers of this section, I can get on with the business of acknowledging people. Rather than save the most important for last, as most writers do, I'll start with them. That's because without my family this book quite literally would not have been possible. I wouldn't have had a thing to write about.

Bryna has commented that life in our family is like living on the set of a sitcom. I pray it never gets canceled. Life with Bryna is a delight and our marriage is a true partnership of love. And somehow she never tires of the words, "Hey, would you read this?"

My sons Benedict and Zachary are a constant source of inspiration, pride, and love. Hopefully nothing in these pages is too embarrassing. And anyway, I'm saving most of my ammunition for your rehearsal dinners.

I am indebted to the parishioners and clergy at the churches I've served: Old St. Paul's in Baltimore, Maryland,

and All Saints' Episcopal Church in Briarcliff Manor, New York. Thanks for allowing me to do the work I have been called to do.

The Rev. Barbara Crafton's initial encouragement and tips on balancing writing with the responsibilities of parish life were, and are, invaluable. I'm also grateful to my editor Cynthia Shattuck for her gentle guidance in shaping this collection. Thank God she has a sense of humor.

I owe much to my mother, Lois Schenck. Her faith and her writing are at the same time inspired and an inspiration. Oh, and thanks for giving birth to me. I have to mention my brother, Matthew Schenck. I'm pretty sure the only way he'll buy a copy of this book is if he sees his name in print. Thanks to a few folks who took time out of their own family chaos to read and comment on some of these essays prior to publication: Elizabeth and Bruce Campbell, Marie and Paul DeCaprio, Susan and Peter Hartzell, and Sharon and JC Mazzola.

A nod to the good folks at Coffee Labs Roasters in Tarrytown, New York, for table space, free refills, doggie treats for Delilah, and caffeine-induced inspiration.

Finally, in no particular order, I'd like to thank some friends and colleagues who have sustained me on my journey thus far: the Rev. Rick Swanson, the Rev. David Cobb, the Rev. Todd McDowell, the Rev. Ann Lovejoy Johnson, the Rev. John Dreibelbis, the Very Rev. Terry White, the Rev. David Knight, the Rev. Bill Van Oss, the Rev. Rob Stevens, the Rev. Patrick Ward, the Rev. Jim Crowder, the Rev. Janice Gordon, the Seabury 9, Neva Rae Fox and all the Episcopal Communicators, and everyone at Seabury-Western Theological Seminary who took turns holding Ben during his first year of life.

FOREWORD

Barbara C. Crafton

"This is going to be good," I thought as I opened the envelope in which the manuscript of this book arrived, and that's about as nice a tribute as a writer can receive. We all want to be writers whose work is anticipated with advance delight.

But really, what's not to like? I've smiled at Tim Schenck's columns for some time now, enjoying his wit, dry but always gentle. He's funny about his kids, but never at their expense. When we meet them, we are meeting our younger selves, and we meet their father as well, bemused, bewildered, and bedeviled in ways we know well.

Jesus talked about family life all the time.

Jealous siblings, harried mothers, perplexed fathers of foolish sons—these first relationships are the crucible in which personality is formed, and they are built to last. And built to teach—the things of God reach our hearts most truly when they are robed in flesh. The God who came to us first as a baby who would grow into a little boy, who would become an impulsive adolescent, who would become a passionate young man, who would never become an old man—this God is soaked in our reality, all its fearsome joy and sorrow.

Tim Schenck watches his children and sees his God. God is in the very dailiness of life, in the tug of ordinary love at the heart. All human love bears the unmistakable imprint of the divine love that brings it all forth.

Introduction: Kids, Chaos, and the Spiritual Life

I don't lead a particularly contemplative life. This may shock anyone who believes members of the clergy lead "stained glass" lifestyles. I don't begin the day with half an hour of silent prayer. More typically it begins with a half-hour argument over getting dressed. The spiritual arc of our family's "morning devotions" has one goal: getting the boys out the door and onto the school bus. Sometimes this happens effortlessly, with little angst and at low volume. Okay, this has never happened. But Bryna and I will be empty nesters in another dozen years, so all in due time.

My house is loud. It is chaotic, joyful, and frenzied. With two boys in elementary school, two multi-tasking parents, a dog, and a goldfish, monastic silences don't exist. Well, maybe for our goldfish, Clem. Yet God is very much in the midst of it all. The chaos doesn't make it any less holy. I've just come to see and appreciate God's presence in new ways. God doesn't just speak to us when we're on our knees, thank God. Otherwise a lot of us would go pretty long in-between conversations.

But it took me awhile to get to this point. The birth of my first child, Benedict, the summer before my last year of seminary, drove a wedge straight through the heart of my spiritual life. The moment the obstetrician directed me to cut the umbilical cord, I unknowingly said good-bye to regular times of worship and prayer. If Ben spit up on me just as I was walking out the door to the seminary chapel (and he invariably did), so much for worship. Ditto if he was napping (you don't make the mistake of waking a sleeping baby more than once). This dramatic transformation of lifestyle and its impact upon the way I approached God took quite a period of adjustment. How could I possibly remain spiritually rooted and "plugged in" when I was being literally and metaphorically tugged at? When Zachary was born twenty months later, I discovered just how quiet things were around the house with only one child. But by then it was too late to enjoy.

All of us go through transitions in life. We move away, get married, have children; we get hired and fired; relationships bloom and fracture. Flexibility may be the ultimate spiritual virtue. Because if we wait until things calm down in our lives before seeking to forge a fruitful relationship with the divine, it will never happen. God's voice and presence is everywhere, even in the midst of the chaos that so often defines our lives.

Eventually I realized that through the chaos of having young children, God opened my eyes to new possibilities and new ways of experiencing the divine. Finding God in the midst of domestic chaos was a revelation that relationship with God can be a very messy affair. And that's okay. God is just as present in our lives when we walk around the block in pajamas at 2:00 a.m. with a crying baby as in a reflective ten minutes of silence before a worship service. The trick is balance. And recognizing that there is no ordinary time; it is all blessed by God.

In ordained ministry, life with young children brings perspective. It's hard to have a "God complex" when your kids expect you to play "garbage truck" every night. They've since outgrown this game of me lying on the floor as the boys stuffed trucks, action figures, and plastic dinosaurs into my shirt. When the garbage truck got full to the point of overflowing, I would go to the town dump by standing up. This would then be repeated ad nauseam. On any given day, I might find myself absolving sins in the name of the church one moment and serving the cause of waste management the next. So much for clerical elitism. There are days I think how much easier life would have been if I'd just entered a monastery. I haven't read the latest theological treatise, I can't imagine getting away for a silent retreat anytime soon, and I can't even stay awake to watch the eleven o'clock news. But the rewards of parenting and living a life of domestic chaos outweigh any inconveniences or lack of sleep. I know far more about love and forgiveness. I recognize that watering the garden with a fussy baby is a form of prayer. And I recognize ever more clearly my own limitations and utter reliance upon God.

I once saw a bumper sticker that read, THERE IS NO SEC-ULAR WORLD. I'm not big on bumper sticker theology— HONK IF YOU LOVE JESUS and the like—but this proclamation said it all. There *is* no secular world. It is all sacred because God pervades everything. This is the guiding premise of the reflections that follow. The divine presence weaves its way throughout our daily lives. God can be found in the miraculous and the mundane; in a family room fish tank, through a child's probing questions, or at the town pool.

I hope you find these pages helpful on your continu-ing journey of life and faith. We are all companions on the way and I hope you'll allow me to accompany you on this brief leg. I invite you to set the pace—these reflections stand alone or may be read in concert with one another. But I do hope you'll join me in laughter and devotion, in love and awe, in seeking and wondering.

I never did catch a glimpse of the driver with that bumper sticker. He or she turned off before I could peek into the window. But it doesn't matter. We often see snippets of the truth on the highways and byways of life, just as we do in the midst of domestic chaos. We simply need to open our eyes to the possibilities.

The Good, the Bad, and the Goldfish

The cosmic battle between good and evil recently raged in our family room. Specifically, within the confines of our fish tank. When Ben was three and a half, he received two goldfish for Christmas. And for the first time in his life he was given the great responsibility of naming living creatures. After talking him out of his first choice of "Yuck" and "P.U.," we ended up with fish named "Good" and "Bad." Ben was in that stage of life where everything is black and white—there are no shades of gray. In those days our house was full of "bad guys" and "good guys" with no moral in-between. It was that simple.

And with our new fish I admit I saw an intriguing possibility, an opportunity to resolve the epic struggle between good and bad once and for all. The only remaining question was Who would prevail? The forces of good or bad? And to think this would all take place within a tiny tank of water in our house. But in the meantime, the fish seemed healthy as they adjusted to their new home, oblivious to the grave matter at stake.

Things were moving along swimmingly until we noticed a couple of dark spots on Bad's gills. They were barely perceptible in the beginning. But as time went on, I became worried. I'm no veterinarian, but Bad seemed to be going from bad to worse. Mercifully, it was quick.

Three days after Christmas, Bad floated to the top of the tank. Good had conquered Bad—which was both good and bad. Because in three short days, we had all become attached to our new pets.

And then there was the question of how to break the news to Ben. It was close to bedtime when Bad breathed his last and Bryna and I debated the options in hushed tones. In a panic, my first thought was to ignore the situation, hope Ben didn't notice, and then rush out to find a replacement for Bad first thing the next morning. A variation on the old bait-and-switch routine.

As the possibilities swirled through our minds, Ben approached us and calmly announced, "Bad died." We both went toward the tank and reluctantly confirmed Ben's diagnosis. With Ben's help, I reverently scooped Bad out of the tank. We went to the first-floor powder room, Ben placed the corpse in the toilet, I said a prayer for Bad, and Ben flushed him down to his final resting place.

Immediately following the burial, Ben went to the stereo and asked me to put on some "baby music." I did so. He then told me that since Bad was a baby, he thought he should hear baby music as he went to Jesus. He also told me the music would help Good since he was lonely and missed Bad. Children do have an amazing sensitivity to ritual.

Bad did not die in vain. That night we spoke of heaven and the nature of mortality and Ben continued to ask questions and began to absorb the notion of death. And in light of a household tragedy, connections were being made in a young mind between life and death, the eternal and the temporal. The passing of a goldfish named Bad helped Ben begin to see how the human experience fits into the story of faith. It also eased the transition into a conversation I really didn't know how to begin. The next day, we did get a new companion for Good. We were discussing potential names and after Ben rejected my idea of having Good and Plenty, he decided on Clementine. Why? Because I happened to be eating one at the time. So we now have Good and Clem. They both seem to be thriving, eating well, and getting along famously. And while the cosmic battle that raged in our house for three days is over, we'll never forget Bad. Ben still asks about him occasionally and we talk about life and death. It is, of course, a lifelong conversation, but I thank Bad for allowing us to get it started.

The Sound of Silence

There's not much silence in our house. If the boys aren't doing battle in their Ninja costumes, they're whining about the injustice of bath night. And if they're not playing football in the family room, they're laughing hysterically over fake burps. Kids don't come with mute buttons. I've looked.

Most of the noise is simply the sound of being a parent with active children. It's our family soundtrack, in a sense; the background "music" of this particular stage of life. It can be deafening at times, but it's so often joyful as well. Nonetheless, moments of silence are essential to our individual sense of well-being and sanity. And few of us, let alone parents of small children, get nearly enough of it. By the time the kids finally fall asleep, Bryna and I are usually too exhausted to enjoy it, and the next thing we know, the sun's starting to rise and Zack's clamoring for breakfast.

Maybe I'm overly sensitive to the lack of silence in our lives, but one thing that drives me nuts is the presence of televisions in public places. They're in airports, auto garages, grocery stores, restaurants, and doctors' offices. Perhaps it makes sense since the average American home now has more televisions than people. But between televisions and iPods, we're surrounded by near constant noise. And it begs the question, what are we afraid of?

Why can't we sit in silence while the mechanic rotates the tires on our SUV? When we find time for silence, even just a small amount, amazing things can happen. Parents may have to trade off with one another to go for a walk in the woods, but then again, silence is best experienced alone anyway. It certainly can't be found at the zoo or the playground or Chuck E. Cheese's.

I remember an ad for a long-forgotten bath product whose slogan was "Calgon, take me away." It showed a stressed-out mother tuning out the sounds of household chaos and slipping into a soothingly warm bubble bath. We all have days (or weeks or months) when we need to be "taken away," and intentional moments of silence can help transport us to a place of tranquility. Even if the first five minutes are spent going over the list for our next Target run or thinking through all the things to do at the office. Unless you're the Dalai Lama (and who is?), you probably can't build several hours of silent meditation into your daily schedule. But even a few moments help. If you're in the car without kids for some reason, turn off the radio. Or, if you're like me, turn off the Barney music that's been playing for the last ten minutes before you even noticed it was on.

Silence played an important role in my own call to ordained ministry, which actually took place over a sustained period of time. I grew up in the Episcopal Church, and when I was in fifth grade, I felt very drawn to the priesthood. This lasted for a little while until I realized I would have to actually get up in front of people and speak. So I dropped the idea. Or at least it went latent for fifteen years. For a few years after college, I found myself working on and managing political campaigns across the country. Now, this work is all-consuming—seven days a week, crazy hours until election day. There's no time for yourself, let alone any time to be quiet. Then you're unemployed for a while until you find the next campaign—there's always one somewhere.

I did this for about four years before I eventually burned out. Or if I didn't burn out, I started to question the way people are used and treated as stepping-stones rather than as children of God. So my sense of call started to resurface. And after leaving politics, I actually had some time to think; some time to listen. One of the things I did after leaving the campaign business was to work for a few months for a contractor. It was mostly basic painting jobs and I always worked alone. So I'd be up on a ladder with time to be with my own thoughts for the first time in years. I was forced to leave space for God and God spoke to me. Not out of a paint can but simply through the process of turning everything off and listening. Something I highly recommend doing on a regular basis, even if it takes some serious spousal negotiating.

At this point, silence in our house is a bad omen. When all I can hear is the hum of the refrigerator, I know the boys are up to no good. That parental sixth sense kicks in, and I usually find them doing an "art" project on their bedroom walls. And then it's my own voice that breaks the silence.

Drive-Thru Window

Every time I drive past a McDonald's, Ben and Zack plead with me to pull over. "We want Happy Meals!" comes the chant from the backseat. Parents know all about Happy Meals—and the persistent nagging they bring out in our children. The power of a cheap plastic toy and overpriced processed chicken is amazing. But within a day or two, the toy inevitably winds up on the floor of the minivan or the family room, forgotten and broken. So perhaps they should be renamed "*Temporarily* Happy Meals." Because the joy lasts only until the toy breaks, the boys get hungry again, and we pass yet another McDonald's.

We have a bucket full of old Happy Meal toys in our house. They're made up almost entirely of toys from old Disney or Pixar films. So there's Buzz Lightyear without a head and Lightning McQueen missing his rear axle. And those are just some of the ones I can identify—there are numerous animals and monsters from movies that flopped. The bucket is a veritable graveyard of animated creatures. What's amazing is the number of places where you can find these characters. How could a child possibly be expected to brush his teeth without Spiderman toothpaste? Or wear a diaper without Elmo's smiling face plastered all over it? Or eat fruit snacks not shaped like Shrek? It's amazing to think that any of us made it to adulthood.

And this has nothing to do with the fact that our parents never even heard of bicycle helmets and that we spent long car trips sprawled out on the backseat with nary a booster seat in sight. All we had were Flintstone vitamins—which means that we quite literally grew up in the Stone Age.

Why is buying SpongeBob ice cream even an option? Because advertising works. Just ask any parent who's gone to the grocery store with a young child. I find that shopping carts turn my kids into octopi—their tentacles reach out longingly for anything they've ever seen on TV. At our house, Zack is particularly susceptible to the lure of advertising. Granted it has something to do with his age, but Mr. Instant Gratification, as I like to call him, wants everything he sees on television and he wants it *now*! Needless to say, he's often disappointed. Besides the fact that we'd quickly go into debt—his desires range from Lucky Charms cereal to a Nintendo Wii to a "real" castle— he may as well learn sooner than later that he can't, in fact, have it all. But boy are there some tantrums that lay between his fantasy and life's reality.

Every parent wants enduring happiness for their children, not just the temporary kind. Sustainable joy doesn't come from a Happy Meal or any other impulse buy. The root of all joy is faith in God, not the next hot toy. Which is also important for adults to remember. It's just as easy for us to fall into the "Happy Meal Syndrome." We see something we want and, believing it will bring us great joy, we go out and get it. And the new sofa or new car or new pair of shoes or new relationship *does* fill us with joy, temporarily. But the delight is transitory and soon forgotten; the happiness is fleeting and we are again left with the same hunger for joy and fulfillment. Then, like a child passing the next McDonald's, we pass another store window or open the next catalog, and the whole cycle starts over again.

The good news is that, when it comes to our children, we do have the power to break this cycle. We can say "no." Which may make us temporarily unpopular and it might mean enduring some powerful backseat whining when we drive past the next fast-food restaurant or toy store. But the whims of children cannot drive our household budgets and family priorities. Seven-year-olds don't need iPods and cell phones. Really.

It may be difficult to ignore the constant nagging. Especially when it's so intense that it makes you want to yank your hair out by the roots. But better that than raising children who will become unfulfilled adults, unable to maintain a life-sustaining relationship with Jesus Christ. Because that's what this is ultimately all about. It's about reordering our priorities to keep God, and nothing else, at the center.

Of course, I still occasionally pull over and get the boys their Happy Meals. Rewards are one of the joys of life for both kids and adults. But as I lean over and steal a few of their French fries, I think about how much of parenting, like life, is a balancing act. And how not everything that makes us "happy" in the short-term offers long-term fulfillment.

I like to eat a Big Mac about once every five years or so. I always feel a bit ill afterward and spend the next thirty miles of a long car trip regretting the decision. But boy, does it taste good at the time. Just like the abundance of emotional and spiritual junk food that exists in the world. Things, like trashy novels or the latest New Age healing method, that taste good going down but are never truly fulfilling. A little bit's okay, of course. Which means I'm about due for another Big Mac.

Deer X-ing

I used to like deer. Growing up in cities, there was a woodsy mystery associated with them. If I encountered one, I was fairly certain Little Red Riding Hood wouldn't be far behind. And seeing that graceful silhouette on a bright yellow DEER X-ING sign usually meant I was on vacation.

Then I moved to suburban Westchester County, New York. It's not that the myth was instantly shattered. I remember how my heart leapt the first time I saw deer in our backyard. I called the kids over to the window and we stared in awe at the beautiful creatures. Bryna, a Westchester native, laughed at me. For some reason she didn't share my wonder. "Just wait," she said.

That fall, our first in Westchester, I planted about seventy-five bulbs. Tulips, to be precise. I chose all sorts of colors: reds and purples, oranges and pinks. There was simply too much green in the yard for my taste, so I decided to take measures into my own hands.

Now, I'm a pretty lousy gardener. When it comes to plants, my major claim to fame is doing the impossible: I managed to kill a cactus. It turns out that they actually do need *some* water. But nevertheless I labored over an entire weekend, carefully choosing the locations, rearranging flowerbeds, digging holes, and gently placing the bulbs into the earth. How pleased I was envisioning the splash of color that would arrive come spring. It wasn't until mid-April that I realized my horticultural foolishness. I didn't realize I had planted deer food. I didn't realize my autumn project would become a spring snack. And suddenly deer were no longer so cute. Instead of calming me, Psalm 42 now made my blood boil: "As the deer longs for the water-brooks, so longs my soul for you, O God." Because it was my tulips the deer seemed to long for. I began glaring and muttering at the deer under my breath. They just stared back, mocking my attempts to cultivate a colorful garden.

As everyone around here knows, and as I've recently learned, the Westchester County deer population is notorious. If they're not spreading Lyme disease through ticks, they're chomping on flowers and causing traffic accidents.

I guess I shouldn't complain. My efforts did result in one tulip. It was a beautiful purple and white flower. Lonely, maybe, but majestic and defiant. Why had this one survived when all the others had been so ruthlessly devoured? I was having these profound thoughts when Zack, who was then two years old, triumphantly plucked off the petals with great enthusiasm and bravado. Oh well.

But maybe we can learn something from these suburban raiders. Not everything conforms to our human wishes. We don't "own" nature and we don't "own" the world that surrounds us. Of course we act as if we do. Isn't that why we tend so compulsively to our manicured lawns? It gives us a sense of order and control. By some estimates Americans spend $61 billion on lawn care each year in attempting to tame the untamable. Because if even the most finely tended lawn in the neighborhood was left alone for a few months, it would quickly revert back to its natural chaotic state.

When I was a kid, my parents had the worst lawn in the neighborhood. Not because of neglect (mowing the lawn was my *least* favorite chore), but because of overuse. All the neighborhood kids played in *our* yard—tag, baseball, you name it. And my parents loved this. But the end result was that our lawn had more dirt than grass. And in a culture of competitive gardening, that made us suspect. Even to some of the parents who encouraged their kids to play on the Schencks' lawn.

The greatest contrast in lawn care was our house and the one just behind it. A retired federal judge lived there. It was the largest house in the neighborhood, and his team of lawn care professionals was unparalleled. When they arrived, it looked like a SWAT team moving out for action. They poured out of their trucks wearing sunglasses and matching uniforms armed with high-powered lawn care weaponry to attack the encroachment of nature. It was a rare occurrence to see even a single leaf on the judge's golf course greens–like lawn. Even at the height of autumn. And I remember after Hurricane David blew through Baltimore in 1979 and two giant oak trees came crashing down on the judge's lawn, it was spotless by the next day. In contrast, whenever it was my turn to mow our lawn, I was just happy when I didn't run over the bright orange cord and electrocute myself.

At least there were no deer in the neighborhood where I grew up. But maybe I should be a bit more sensitive. After all, it was suburban sprawl that led to the displacement of these animals in Westchester County. So maybe the aggravating deer population is a healthy thorn in our side, reminding us that there are indeed some things beyond control in this life. Not a bad message for us to ponder. I certainly have a better idea of who's in charge around here. And it's neither the deer nor me.

What Size Are God's Shoes?

What does God look like? This question gets asked a lot at our house and I never have a very good answer. I tend to mutter something about us being made in God's image. And then, once the boys have expressed adequate annoyance at my unsatisfying answer, what follows is a steady stream of more probing questions about God's appearance. They're relentless—like sharks who've smelled blood. "How tall is God? Does God have a face? How big are God's hands? Does God have really big shoes?" On and on they come, making me feel less and less adequate as a parent and as a member of the clergy. Because my answers can't possibly be complete.

Sometimes I turn the question around and ask, "What do *you* think God looks like?" This is a classic counseling technique, redirecting the unanswerable into a question. And, while I'm never too proud to use it on my kids, it doesn't work. Often I end up in the land of generalities by stating that God is everywhere. Which is true but not exactly the most concrete answer. I think this response in particular, the one about God being everywhere, leads to the obsession with God's size. If God is everywhere, the next logical question may well be to wonder about the immense size of God's shoes.

The fact is, we don't know what God looks like. We haven't a clue. Scripture certainly gives us lots of *images* of God. But I can't really tell the boys that God is a rock or a whirlwind or fire. We're told that we're made in the image of God, but that doesn't really help us too much. Is that literal or metaphorical? And getting into an existential debate with a four-year-old is a road to nowhere. Believe me, I've tried.

But ultimately, does it matter what God looks like? For humans, seeing is often believing. And so, for many, that's the end of the conversation. "If I can't see something, I can't believe in it. End of story." It's "Doubting" Thomas without the chance to touch Jesus' wounds and believe. To know what something or someone looks like is a way to gain control or power over that thing. If we can visualize something, then we can describe it with our own words. And if we can see it and name it, we somehow own it. But God is too great to be contained by human sight or language. So we can never fully see God or describe God in totality. And we certainly can't own God.

We can, however, *experience* God. And this happens in all sorts of ways. We can experience God through the compassion and love of others. We can experience God through the majesty of nature. We can experience God simply by wondering alongside a child about God's appearance.

When I was a little boy, my family had a children's Bible. I have no idea where it is at this point; I haven't seen it in years. But I vividly remember the inside cover. It had an illustration of a brilliant, multicolored star stretching over the entire length of the page. My parents, probably out of desperation or exasperation from the unceasing questions, suggested that maybe that was God.

And the image has stuck with me throughout my life. Not as the definitive image of what God looks like but as one possibility. Somehow it beats George Burns. As I'm faced with question after question about what God looks like, I find myself answering "yes" to most of these questions. Is God tall? Yes, and short too. Does God have big shoes? Yes, and small ones too. Because the fullness of God is the ultimate "yes." If God is in everything, then God is both tall and short, big and small, and every size in-between. God has a face and yet God does not have a face. God is a tree or a flower or a star and yet God is so much more than any of these.

John's gospel tells us simply that "God is love." It's a straightforward statement, a three-word sentence. "God is love." And maybe *that's* what God looks like: love. It may be an elderly couple holding hands, a mother cradling her child, the sharing of tears with a grieving friend. Love comes in many forms and appears in many faces. And so does God.

For Christians, the most tangible face of God is, of course, Jesus himself. In the face of Jesus, we see God. If God is love, Jesus personifies that love. His face is the very face of God because it is the very face of love. And so whenever we serve the poor, feed the hungry, or clothe the naked, we not only share God's love, we see it.

But of course, none of this provides the most tangible answer for a child wanting to know if God is tall. So I keep saying "yes" to the onslaught of questions and I do what I can to be a loving father. For if God is love, then we see God by showing our love for others. We see the face of God in one another. Our faces can reflect the love that is God. You and I can look like God, if only occasionally, if only briefly, if only haltingly. But we have the ability to do this precisely because we are made in God's image.

I'm not sure what size sandals Jesus wore. A ten? An eleven wide? I assume no one ever measured his "footprints in the sand." But it probably doesn't matter. Because there's a wideness in experiencing God's all-encompassing love and mercy.

The Power of the Dark Side

Ben has turned to the dark side. Maybe it was inevitable—all his friends are Yankee fans. But still I held out hope before we moved to New York from Baltimore when he was three. When he turned six, he anointed Derek Jeter his new hero. And, to my thinking, this is pure heresy.

It could have been different. When he was young and impressionable, I taught him to say, "Boo Yankees, go Orioles" at the mere mention of the Bronx Bombers. I always viewed raising a Yankee-hating Oriole fan as a critical piece of my parental duty. And I've failed. All the love in the world doesn't excuse this calamity. To make things worse, Ben has corrupted Zack. So the insidious virus continues to spread throughout our home.

I had reservations about moving to New York. When I left my position as the assistant priest at a church in downtown Baltimore to become rector of a church in Westchester County I told Bryna, a native New Yorker, that if either of our boys became Yankee fans, we would immediately move and send them to pinstripe detox. But here we are, living in New York, with no moving vans in sight.

The boys are obsessed with Star Wars. And maybe there's a parallel here. Anakin Skywalker, a Jedi knight, moved to the dark side of the Force to become Darth Vader. My boys have undergone a similar metamorphosis.

Albeit without the annoying heavy breathing. They've moved from the light of Birdland to the darkness of the Evil Empire. They've become my own personal fallen angels. And it's painful to watch.

I recently took Ben to his first game at Yankee Stadium to see the Yanks take on the Orioles. I donned my well-worn O's cap. He wore the Yankee hat his mother bought him in open defiance against my household ban on all things Yankee. We held hands walking up the ramp into the stadium, a picture of conflicting loyalties. I assured him the Orioles would win. He stuck his tongue out at me and reminded me how much shorter I was than Randy Johnson.

The game itself was brutal. In between Ben's diet of hot pretzels, cotton candy, and ice cream, the Yankees trounced the Orioles 12–2. So now I'm raising an arrogant Yankee fan (as if there's any other kind) who believes winning is his birthright. I'll have to find another way to teach him humility. I hold out hope he'll start rooting for the Knicks.

I was just about Ben's age when my father took me to my first Orioles game at the old Memorial Stadium. It's since been razed, of course, but my memories have not. The Birds beat the Red Sox that day in 1975. Who knew that exactly thirty years later I'd bring my own son to his first baseball game? For me, it began a lifelong love affair with the game of baseball and the Baltimore Orioles. But even more important was the growing bond between a father and son.

George Steinbrenner has broken ground on a new Yankee Stadium. So Ben won't be able to bring his future children to the place where he saw his first game. And that's too bad. But it's the memories and the relationships that transcend all else. Even, and I cringe when I say this, team loyalties.

We've since gone to an Orioles-Yankees game at Camden Yards in Baltimore. Again, I wore my Orioles gear and both boys wore Yankee caps and Jeter shirts. Bryna donned neutral colors and, like Switzerland, stayed out of the ensuing conflict. The highlight for me (it wasn't the final score) was a visit from the Oriole Bird, the team's mascot. The Bird came over, grabbed Ben's hat, wiped it on both arm pits, put it in his beak, and pretended to throw it back up. Bravo!

Of course there's another lesson in this whole tragic episode besides avoiding a move to the Tri-State area. We don't own or control our children. As much as we seek to protect them and shield them from the evils of life, they need to find their own way. I thank Ben and Zack for this reminder. Even if they unintentionally made the point in the most egregious way imaginable.

Death by Chocolate

I have a confession to make. I don't like chocolate. I'm not allergic to it. It doesn't make me break out in hives. I just don't like it—and in the eyes of most red-blooded Americans, this makes me suspect. When I politely decline a postdinner thin mint or a midday Hershey bar, people give me strange looks. Some literally back away in horror as if they've encountered a leper.

The only person who appreciates this quirk is my chocolate-adoring wife. Granted, Bryna thinks I'm a bit odd, but she relishes the benefits. At Halloween, she competes only with the kids for access to the sugary bounty. If she hears me creaking down the stairs for a midnight snack, she can rest assured that the leftover chocolate cake is safe from my clutches. If she wants to keep me at arm's length, she can just pop a Hershey's Kiss into her mouth. In the grand scheme of things, not getting chocolate on Valentine's Day is a small price to pay.

This abnormality is not a family trait. No therapist would allow me to pin the blame on my mother. The rest of my family indulges in chocolate with reckless abandon. I do think, however, that a childhood experience helped shape this aspect of my culinary personality. Deeply embedded in my psyche is a family trip to Germany's Black Forest. I was probably six or seven at the time. My taste buds had experienced normal development to that point. My tongue was well acquainted with M&Ms and mint chocolate chip ice cream. The problem, I'm increasingly convinced, can be traced to a small bed-and-breakfast in the heart of Germany's cuckoo clock country. Before retiring for the evening, we all found small wrapped chocolates on our pillows. When they were spotted, my brother and I had already brushed our teeth. Mom and Dad quickly deemed them off limits. The next day, breakfast came and went. We climbed into our small, stifling rental car and continued our trek into the heart of the Black Forest. It was the middle of summer and brutally hot. After several hours of this, I started to get hungry. Being stuck in the backseat was also making me slightly queasy, but we all agreed food would help. As we were in the middle of nowhere, we scoured the car for food but found only the chocolates from the night before. I grabbed two or three half-melted mini bars and stuffed them into my mouth.

This was not your average over-sugared American milk chocolate. No, this was bitterly dark German chocolate. Pretty soon, the combination of heat, the motion of the car, and the darkest chocolate ever produced proved a disastrous combination. Dad pulled the car over at my request and my open mouth proceeded to fertilize a small section of the Black Forest.

Since then, the smell of chocolate has made my stomach turn. My worst nightmare is being trapped in Willy Wonka's chocolate factory. I've never had a desire to go to Hershey Park. I cross the street to avoid walking past a Godiva store. I'm fairly certain that the classic dessert "Death by Chocolate" might actually kill me.

I'm not interested in hypnosis to return a taste for chocolate to my palette. It's just not that important to me. I've made peace with my identity as a chocolate hater and the unpopular social ramifications that go along with it. But it is a good reminder of what it means to live a counter-cultural existence. In modern America, people of faith are even more countercultural than people who hate chocolate. Not in a tie-dyed, bell-bottom, Woodstock kind of way but in a world-denying, differing-priorities sort of way. I don't mean to set up a dualistic worldview where things of the spirit are diametrically opposed to things of the flesh. While many religious leaders actively embrace this model, it's a bit simplistic. And it feels like a good-versus-evil superhero model of spirituality.

There are ways, however, in which being faithful does stand in direct opposition to culture. And we're faced with these choices nearly every day. Do I go to church with my family or take my daughter to that soccer game that starts at 10:30 a.m. on Sunday morning? Do I say grace after ordering eggs-over-easy at the diner or skip it for fear of looking like a Jesus freak? Do I give extra money to the homeless shelter or order HBO to go with basic cable? These are all choices we face in our daily walk with the divine. And they lead to many areas of gray in our spiritual lives.

So not eating chocolate while living in a world of choco-holics is a reminder that living a life of faith demands some sacrifice. It means making some hard choices. People won't always agree with your choices, but as long as they're made faithfully and with conviction, you will be rewarded by God.

As for me, I'm a dessert pariah and I've accepted my fate. In the grand scheme of things, it's not much of a cross to bear.

Party Animals

My kids are party animals. Birthday party animals. I swear one of them attends a birthday party every weekend. My social calendar is nowhere near as full. Of course, I don't get party bags full of Nerds, lollipops, and plastic sunglasses. Because that's exactly what kids need after gorging themselves on cake and ice cream: candy for the ride home.

For parents, the general pattern for these parties is pretty standard. Show up at the bowling alley/roller rink/gymnastics center/pizza arcade at the appointed time, put the gift on the designated table, and flee. When children are very young, parents are expected to stick around for the party. So you make small talk with other parents while praying that your child doesn't bite some other kid. But once they reach a certain age, you basically drive past the Taekwondo place and shove your kid out the door while yelling, "Have fun, buddy! See you at 4:30."

The real problem is those parties that take place at the Chuck E. Cheese's thirty minutes from our house. By the time you drive home and eat a snack, you have to turn around and drive right back for pickup. So instead you wander around some mall like a zombie for an hour before returning to watch your kid play one last game of whack-a-mole. And, by the way, Mr. Cheese or whoever invented this place should really be locked up for crimes against humanity, but that's a cause I'll have to pursue on my own time.

The other side of the birthday coin (and given the expense, I mean this literally) is having to host them. We went retro for Ben's eighth birthday party. Or at least it felt that way given the over-programmed parties I've seen. Since when do you need to plan out every single moment of a second grader's time with their friends? We decided to let Ben have four or five of his best friends over to the house for dinner. We had given him a choice of a larger party at a birthday place or a smaller party at home with a bigger present from us. He wisely (and thankfully) chose option number two. But what made the party "retro" is that we didn't plan any activities. Besides ordering pizza and bringing out a cake, the plan was to just let the boys be boys. Just before the kids came over, Bryna did start to get a bit nervous. "Should we come up with at least a few activities?" she wondered. "Nah," I said, "They'll be fine."

And, for once, I was right. For two hours the boys ran amuck in the backyard playing football and baseball, making up nicknames for one another and generally just having some gloriously unstructured time together. Sure, Zack got smacked in the face with a Wiffle ball bat—nothing a bit of ice and a hug from mom couldn't cure in about two minutes. But besides this minor injury, everything went smoothly. And by that I mean there were no trips to the emergency room to dampen the mood.

In our overprotective and litigious culture, the idea of letting boys run around without first having parents sign a waiver would make some adults cringe. But heck, you could always drop a bowling ball on your foot. In fact, Zack was invited to a birthday party at a bowling alley that was cancelled at the last minute because the roof suddenly collapsed. Things happen, and insisting kids wear helmets for every single activity can only afford so much protection. Now, thank God it didn't rain during Ben's party because I'm sure I'd still be twitching from the experience. But it didn't, and the kids had such a good time that some of the other parents have asked us about our "secret" to hosting such a successful party.

Despite the birthday *party* madness, I love celebrating birthdays. Marking a birthday is a wonderful expression of love for someone simply because they exist. Strip away all the recalcitrant piñatas (we once got one that *I* couldn't break open, let alone a bunch of four-year-olds), the balloon-wielding clowns, the Star Wars–themed plates, and you're left with the essence of simplicity: God loves you and we love you for no other reason than because you were born. That should be the underlying premise of every birthday celebration.

Now that doesn't mean I'll be throwing a Jesus-themed party when Zack turns seven. *You* try explaining to him why he won't be having the "Hulk party" he requested. Zack's actually planned out every birthday party theme from now until he turns fifty. Sometime in his mid-forties you may be invited to his Ninja party. But a Jesus-themed party just isn't happening. There would be too many decisions to make: a Judas or Herod piñata? Which tax collectors and sinners would we invite to eat pizza with us? Pin the tail on the Pharisee or Sadducee?

In the meantime, we'll keep hauling the boys to birthday parties all over suburbia. At some point I assume the parties will get smaller and they'll only go to the parties of close friends. At least until the bar mitzvahs kick in.

Aging Out

I noticed my first gray hair this week. It was just a small scraggly thing sticking out from my right temple. Nothing to be alarmed by; a natural sign of aging. Oh, I could blame all sorts of people and things—like my kids or the demands and expectations of parish ministry. But I'm not that concerned about it. Yet. Plus I never saw myself as a "Just for Men" kind of guy.

But the clock is ticking. A few more years and I'll officially become a high-risk candidate for a midlife crisis. I've started gazing longingly at motorcycles even though Bryna would kill me long before I had a chance to maim myself by tipping it over in our driveway. I don't think my lone gray hair is giving me a pre–midlife crisis, but it does give me pause. The aging process is a slippery slope. A gray hair one day leads to back pain, which morphs into arthritis, which leads to a bum hip. Soon enough, I'll be test-driving walkers at the local medical supply shop.

Zack recently announced that he's never going to become a grownup. There is, of course, a classic diagnosis for such cases: Peter Pan Syndrome. It has afflicted generations of children but most successfully grow out of it. Zack says it's "boring" being a grownup because you can't play with toys. Little does he know that they just get smaller, electronic, and much more expensive. But it's true that most grownups he knows don't put on costumes and play Ninja Turtles with one another. They also don't seem to watch Pokemon cartoons or get lollipops from the barber. When they get together, all grownups like to do is talk and eat. Booooring. So from Zack's perspective being an adult appears exceedingly dull.

Aging itself is one sign that our perspective has shifted. It's often imperceptible until a strand of gray hair appears, or you can no longer fit into your normal pant size without writhing on the floor with your legs in the air. Suddenly you notice that standing in line to get Springsteen tickets doesn't seem so important; you can always listen to the CD. Or that you know more about car seat installation than this year's favorites for the Indy 500. But our perspective shifts as we age. Priorities change and we find ourselves in places we'd never dreamed of a few years earlier. Like back-to-school night at our children's elementary school or in bed at 10:00 p.m. on a Saturday night.

Another sign of our changing perspectives is our approach to the stories of the Bible. It's always amazing to me that no matter how many times we've heard a particular passage, it always brims with new insights and revelations. Some of this, I think, has to do with God allowing us to hear what we need to hear at a particular time in our lives. But another reason is that as we age, we encounter new experiences in life. Simply put, our perspective changes. And so the story of Abraham's binding of Isaac, for instance, will sound different to a young boy than it will to that same person when he is a young father or a grandfather.

None of this means that our original perspective was somehow shortsighted or wrong. It just highlights the fact that the life of faith is an evolutionary process and the way we hear God in the present builds upon our cumulative life experiences.

But still, aging is hard. For many of us on the cusp of forty (or any other age-related milestone), the underlying issue is the realization of our own mortality. We're used to feeling and acting as if we're invincible. And the reality that we're not often hits in very personal ways. When I entered my mid-thirties, I realized that if I were a major league baseball player (some fantasies die slow, painful deaths), I would no longer be signed to a multiyear contract. I'd be destined to a series of one-year deals for the rest of my playing career. Fortunately, physical prowess is less important in parish ministry, and my congregation hasn't made any noise about wanting to trade me for a "priest to be named later."

Children themselves are very tangible markers of time. The marks on the wall where we keep our homemade growth chart keep creeping upward. Both boys go through clothes like Imelda Marcos goes through shoes. And it's hard to avoid thinking about your age when you share your home with two age-obsessed and constantly growing creatures. Ben's not "almost eight," he's "seven and 4/5ths" thank you very much. And don't you forget it.

There are still occasional "glory days" moments. Last week I was carded when I bought a case of Heineken while wearing my clerical collar. I politely thanked the cashier. I guess she thought I was using the collar as a ploy. Why didn't I think of that when I was in college? But what I really wanted to do was point to my one gray hair and yell, "Here's my ID, lady!"

Fairness Doctrine

"It's not fair!" Justice is a big theme at our house. Especially when it comes to doling out ice cream ("He got more than me!"), cleaning up toys ("*I* didn't play with Superman, make *him* put it away"), and the care of pets ("I fed Delilah *yesterday*"). This is nothing new; I made the same arguments when I was a kid. And I really *should* have been able to stay up later than my younger brother on school nights.

You can never win the battle over equality between siblings. Even when you use a ruler to measure out equal amounts of strawberry milkshake in each glass, one still claims that he's been shortchanged. I know; I've done this.

As parents, Bryna and I spend an inordinate amount of energy trying to be "fair," while balancing the differing needs of our children. It's a losing cause. Someone always ends up with one more sprinkle on his ice cream sundae. And even if Ben's clearly outgrown his pajamas and Zack's still fit, God forbid if we don't get them both new PJs. Because while they're quick to point out any perceived slight on the scales of justice, they're just as quick to proclaim "I got more than you!" whenever we hand out cheese doodles.

It's interesting that most kids are fairness obsessed yet remain preoccupied with the question, "Who do you love more, him or me?" So at the root of the fairness issue is insecurity. No matter how much you tell them you love them, no matter how much you show them you love them, there's always a shred of doubt that you may not love them enough. Or that you love their brother more. As if love were a commodity you could measure out into equal parts. We do the same thing when we don't recognize that God's love for us is truly unconditional. Oh, we say that it is, but do we really believe it? Do we live our lives in such a way that shows we fully believe that God will love us despite all of our faults? Like our kids, we're secretly worried about getting a raw deal, especially when we compare ourselves to others. "I work just as hard as that guy," we think. "Why is he driving a Lexus and I'm stuck with a used Mercury Tracer?"

The great cliché we use whenever one kid gets invited to a baseball game by his best friend and the other doesn't get to go is, "Life isn't fair." And it's true. We're all unique individuals on distinctive life journeys. As parents, we try to be fair to our kids while giving each one according to his needs. But it's never good enough. And I simply can't spend my days following the boys around wielding a measuring cup and a tape measure. I'd go insane, and not just because I'm lousy with fractions.

Anyway, exact equality shouldn't always be the goal. I'm obviously not going to give Zack a banana split for dessert with all the toppings and hand Ben a piece of burnt toast. That really wouldn't be fair. But fairness doesn't necessarily mean absolute equality. Children are different, and so at times their needs diverge. Zack may need more of my attention in the days leading up to the first day of school; Ben may need a walk with me to figure out what to do about a kid who is being a bully. But you still better count the number of gifts Santa leaves under the tree to make sure the elves were evenhanded this year. Ben and Zack sure do.

Again, fairness doesn't mean that everything need always be equal. Not every kid needs to have exactly fourteen eggs in their baskets following an Easter egg hunt. As long as everyone gets *some*, who cares if a few kids have more than the others? Heck, if you want to see competitive blood sport, you should witness our town egg hunt held on the Saturday before Easter every year. I've seen parents racing around other kids to grab eggs and dump them in their three-year-old's basket so they can "get more" than the other kids. That, of course, is why Jesus died for us: so *your* kid can "win" the egg hunt. But I digress.

Kids may as well learn now that fairness doesn't always mean equality. Unlike in youth sports, adults don't get "participation" trophies for showing up: "Thanks for coming in to the office today, here's a plaque."

Maybe this is why I get so annoyed with bumpers at bowling alleys. It used to be that if you stunk at bowling, you'd roll a gutter ball. It was especially embarrassing to roll one at a birthday party in front of a bunch of your friends, but it forced you to try and bowl straighter in the next frame. I remember receiving a booby prize at a second-grade birthday party when I was a kid for having the worst score. Ah, the humiliation. At the end of the party, the parents of the birthday boy handed me a party bag and my prize: a bag of beer nuts. I've since wondered what kind of parent would possibly give an eight-year-old beer nuts, but whatever. It was the seventies.

With bumpers guarding the gutters, it is now literally impossible to roll a gutter ball. And that's too bad. This makes every kid feel good, I guess, but how will they learn the agony of bowling defeat? And more importantly, how will they earn their beer nuts?

I'll still make sure the boys get an equal number of pitches when we're playing Wiffle ball in the backyard. When I fail to do so, they carry on as if I'd cut them out of the will. But I also want them to know that fairness doesn't always translate into equality. Progress on this front is slow.

Field of Dreams

I can't fully explain why, but I was mystically drawn to the old Memorial Stadium in Baltimore several years ago. The pilgrimage was spurred by the announcement of the structure's imminent destruction at the hands of a wrecking ball. Yes, the stadium had become the latest victim of the building craze in the arena of professional sports that has turned many old stadiums into dinosaurs before their time. Memorial Stadium, the one-time home of the Orioles and Colts had sat vacant for a number of years, falling into disrepair and becoming a mere shell of its former glory. And yet I was drawn back to this place, a place where I spent much of my youth dreaming, rejoicing, despairing, cheering, and jeering.

When the sale of stadium artifacts was announced, an indefinable force propelled me back to 33rd Street. A variation on the mantra from the Kevin Costner baseball movie *Field of Dreams* came to mind: "If you raze it, they will come." As I stood in line with my fellow pilgrims waiting to get onto the field, I couldn't help but feel that I was entering a space no less sacred than a European cathedral ruin. If you've ever experienced this, you know that even though the stained-glass windows are long gone, weeds shoot up through the remains of the stone floor, and bats glide boldly through what's left of the vaulted ceiling, there is still a pervasive sense of being on holy ground. The generations of prayers that emanated from the site still hover like a cloud of witnesses. You can almost hear the voices of the choir lifted to God in praise and glory.

So it was as I walked for the first time onto that glorious field of dreams that was Memorial Stadium. Despite the fact that weeds had overtaken the outfield, the windows of the press box were smashed, and the concrete dugouts were crumbling, I was very much walking on holy ground. In my mind's eye I could see the stadium packed with a cheering throng. The life, energy, and electricity that once pulsed through the place was much more than a distant memory. The hope and excitement of a little boy once again coursed through my veins and I felt as if my adult self had just been introduced to the childhood version.

But I came to the stadium not just in search of memories but as a sojourner seeking a holy relic. Items from the stadium were being sold and I wanted, even needed, one. I had my heart set on a stadium seat, the kind I used to sit in as a boy, a teenager, and a young adult. I sought a tangible piece of this place that I could take home and cherish forever. For Memorial Stadium was more than simply a place where I learned to love the liturgy and ritual of baseball. It was a place of relationships, memories, and magic.

Even more important than my sporting reminisces are the memories of time spent with my father. He took me to my first baseball game in 1975, shortly after my family moved to Baltimore. He had absolutely no interest in the game; he was a symphony orchestra conductor after all, but didn't want to limit my interests because of his own. As it turned out, I fell in love with the stadium and the game of baseball at first sight. And over the years he actually became quite an Orioles fan himself. When he was dying of cancer, he wrote my brother and me a letter while he watched the last Orioles game ever played at Memorial Stadium. In it he wrote about his love for us and the sense of peace he felt as he prepared to take leave of this world. He died several months after the final out was recorded, and I've always associated the death of Memorial Stadium with the death of my father. Its final destruction was like one last shovelful of dirt being thrown over my earthly relationship with him. I mourn the loss of the stadium, as I do the loss of my father, but I also take comfort in having known them both.

During the Orioles' American League pennant-winning season of 1979, the string of improbable, come-from-behind, last-minute victories led to the coining of the slogan "Miracle on 33rd Street." I think the real miracle is that God brought together so many people through the steel, concrete, and brick that made up Memorial Stadium. God touched my soul and nurtured my family, as well as countless others, through a public, "secular" structure. Christ's incarnation is indeed all-pervasive.

Well, I now have my stadium seat. To Bryna's chagrin it sits in our family room, though she did manage to keep it out of the living room. I'm not entirely sure what drove me to seek out a piece of the stadium. But I do know that it's comforting to have in the house. If a religious icon is a window into the mystery of the divine, my new chair is a kind of icon. It serves as a window into a special time in my life and it somehow puts me in touch with a part of my heart that I will always cherish.

Pack Mules

I've become the person I used to laugh at in airports. Traveling light is an oxymoron when you travel with children. The single carry-on bag is a distant memory. Bryna and I trudge through Concourse B with tremendous amounts of baggage. We push strollers and luggage carts, we carry car seats and diaper bags, and generally look and feel like pack mules. That haggard look on our faces as we return from another "relaxing" vacation makes us resemble fleeing refugees. Perhaps this is what Jesus was referring to when he said, "Come to me, all you that are weary and carrying heavy burdens" (Matthew 11:28). I'd love it if he would at least grab the Pack 'n Play for me.

I can't help but contrast our mode of travel with Jesus' guidelines for the seventy missionaries he sent out as messengers to spread the good news of God's kingdom. It's a high calling; an important task. And it must have been worthy of great amounts of luggage. But Jesus doesn't see it this way. They're allowed the clothes on their back. That's it. More than anything else, Jesus gives them an antipacking list: "Take no gold, or silver, or copper in your belts, no bag for your journey, or two tunics, or sandals or a staff" (Matthew 10:9–10).

The way most of us pack for even an overnight trip makes this mode of travel nearly inconceivable. And it's not just the physical stuff we haul around—the toiletries, the extra shoes, the credit cards. We tend to metaphorically overpack on this journey of life and faith. And it's this metaphorical baggage that is even heavier than our overstuffed suitcases. We carry great loads of spiritual and emotional baggage. Items from our past; worries about the future that weigh us down. And it's hard work lugging this stuff around.

So why does Jesus tell his co-laborers to "carry no purse, no bag, no sandals"? In a sense, he's trying to teach them survival techniques. Not like *Gilligan's Island* or *Survivor*, but the true essentials of life. We don't need all the stuff. We don't need to carry around extra baggage. Faith in Jesus Christ is sufficient.

By demanding that the seventy forsake anything extraneous, they are forced to remain focused on the task at hand. But perhaps more importantly, they are forced to trust in God. It's easy to talk about trusting God when we cling to all sorts of security blankets like money and possessions and houses. But forsaking all else brings us to a new level of trust. There are enough distractions for us without adding extra baggage to our individual and collective journeys.

Admittedly this is easier said than done. I couldn't imagine leaving for a family vacation and simply trusting that snacks will appear when the boys get hungry. Or that an affordable, yet clean, place to stay will show up when we're ready to sleep. But this is in effect what Jesus demands of us. If we are encumbered with baggage, it is impossible to fully follow Christ. In response to Jesus' words, "Follow me," we can't say, "Hold on, let me pack my suitcase." We just go.

Jesus doesn't say it's going to be easy. In fact, just the opposite: he says, "I am sending you out like sheep into the midst of wolves" (Matthew 10:16). It will not always be a smooth journey. There will indeed be obstacles to encounter and overcome in this life. You may miss your connecting flight. You may wind up sitting in the airport for five hours. Your flight may be cancelled altogether. But you keep going because God urges us onward, to complete the journey that is set before us.

After telling those who are "heavy laden" to come to him, Jesus goes on to say that he will "refresh" them and that his "yoke is easy and his burden light." The very image of a yoke is one of great weight. And Bryna and I feel like yoked beasts of burden walking up to the ticket counter at LaGuardia. But Jesus turns this image upside down. Which is something he does a lot for us: a stable is transformed into a palace; the marginalized poor into the blessed; the cross from an implement of death into an instrument of new life. And so there's no reason why the heavy yoke of discipline can't be transformed into a freeing symbol of joy.

One day the kids will be able to tote their own stuff. One day I'll no longer need to consider them flight risks in public places. One day I won't spend an entire flight pleading with Zack to stop kicking the seat in front of him. And hopefully one day they'll learn to travel light through this life, relying solely on their faith to carry them on the journey.

Handyman's Special

The worst grade I ever got was in my sixth-grade shop class. All my classmates loved shop. It was a welcome break from geography and grammar and to them it was a treat. Trading textbooks for goggles and desks for circular saws approached nirvana. They loved the walk down into the basement where the shop was located. It was a magical place so unlike any other at school. The smell of sawdust and the distinct noise of the jig saw made it clear that this was a place where things were built. For sixth-grade boys, it was a manly haven. The machines were huge and there were so many of them. It looked like dad's basement workshop gone wild.

For me the weekly trip to shop class was a journey into a torturous dungeon. It wasn't that I worried about losing an arm, or that I feared the tools—I thought they were as cool as the next kid. And it wasn't even the icy stare of the perpetually grumpy shop teacher whose oft-repeated mantra was "The shop is not a playground."

The problem for me was a space just off the shop called the drafting room. That's what terrified me. Because in the drafting room we were expected to draw the objects we were to build. And this combined all of my academic weaknesses: drawing and math. Oh, I could have drawn a fine *abstract* toolbox. I could have written a clever essay about the life of a toolbox. I just couldn't ever draw a toolbox to scale.

None of this has changed over the years, and I'm still terrible with tools. Jesus may have been a carpenter, but none of his skills ever rubbed off on me. I look at houses being built in my town, usually the McMansion variety, and I wonder where you would even begin. Dig a hole? Buy a bunch of wood? In Matthew 21:42, Jesus is called the "cornerstone" of our faith. That makes sense to me—he's the foundation upon which all else is built. And while I can relate to it metaphorically, I'd never be able to tell you why this particular stone is so critical to a masonry structure. But if Jesus is the cornerstone, what does that make us? How do we fit into the overall building design? Yes, I'm staying in the realm of metaphor—I tend to do that when I don't have a clue about something.

The mistake we so often make is to view ourselves as the builders. We see ourselves as the masters of our own destinies, the creators of our own kingdoms. But we're not the architects or the well-heeled developers; we're not even the builders when it comes to that. You and I are the bricks. That's our role in this whole thing. We're essential to the overall structure, but we don't choose where we'll be placed or how we'll function in the big picture of the design.

It's not always glamorous to be a brick. We don't command individual attention. When you look at a house, you don't notice the individual bricks, you notice the whole structure. We're part of something larger, but by ourselves we're not the entire structure. We're not the foundation, we're not the cornerstone; we're the bricks.

You've probably seen one of those "buy-a-brick" fundraisers. They crop up when new walkways are built in communities or around schools or museums. I actually "own" a brick in Baltimore as a result of one of these. In 1990, the city ran one of these programs in the historic Fell's Point neighborhood. My parents couldn't think of anything for stocking stuffers one year, so they gave me and my brother bricks with our names on them. They didn't jam the actual brick into our stockings, of course, but a certificate of authenticity. Mine's on a walkway that goes out onto a public pier. We never were able to locate Matt's, but every time I visit Baltimore I like to find mine. It's faded over the years, but my name is clearly visible. It always takes me a little while to find it, since I can never remember its precise location. But I always find it, wipe off any bird poop, and stare at it for a moment before moving on. The boys like to hop up and down on it.

I think we like to know that there is something permanent about our lives. Which is why people invest in huge marble tombstones. Of course, my brick will one day crumble. The pathway will be dug up and replaced, perhaps with new bricks and the names of others. But as a brick that is permanently affixed to the cornerstone of our faith, we're part of a magnificent structure that will never be razed or imploded.

Bryna still gets nervous every time I take out the drill around the house. My usual ratio is two extraneous holes for every correct one. Nothing a well-placed picture can't hide. But thankfully, when it comes to our spiritual lives, we don't have to draw up the plans or use the tools. All we have to do is let God use us as the building material that we are. We are the bricks, and that's not a bad thing.

God Is My Superhero

"God is stronger than the Hulk." This may not be profound theology, but I assume it's true and I affirm this belief on a regular basis. Ben and Zack are consumed with questions about God and they're also enamored with superheroes. This leads to numerous comparisons between the powers of God and the powers of superheroes. Is God faster than a speeding bullet? Sure. Is God able to leap tall buildings in a single bound? Absolutely. Such is life at the intersection of the supernatural and the superhuman.

In our house, God has become the standard by which all superheroes are measured. The Hulk may be strong, but God is even stronger. Batman may be smart, but God is even smarter. God is the ultimate superhero. No caped crusader can approach God's mighty power.

I'm not particularly proud of my superhero theology. It's simplistic, speculative, and rooted in fantasy. But I'm just trying to show that God is beyond anything we can know or imagine. And if there's anything that Ben and Zack know, it's superheroes. They've got them all—even relatively obscure ones like Flash and Aquaman—and they play with them all the time. Some of the quietest moments at our house take place when both boys have their own superhero battles going on in their respective rooms. I love hearing those barely audible attacking noises of independent, engaged play. Partly because the sound of high-pitched mayhem is just so darned cute, but mostly because it's much more civilized than the battles that take place when the boys play superheroes together. This is usually okay until Spiderman and Superman start in on one another instead of fighting a common enemy. Suddenly they're arguing about whether Spiderman's webs can contain Superman or whether Superman can use his X-ray vision to uncover Spiderman's secret identity, among other esoteric questions of superhero ability. Then it devolves into brotherly warfare.

But I think the allure of superheroes also speaks to the powerful sense of comfort and protection they offer. Let's face it, they never lose. This may be particularly important as they begin to realize that their parents are, well, human. I've tried to hide this from them as long as possible, but cracks are starting to appear in the façade. I sometimes burn the hamburgers when I cook on the grill; I really don't have *any* idea why the sky is blue; and my jokes can evidently be embarrassing when used in front of classmates. Who knew? So while I'm clearly no superhero in the boys' eyes, at least I don't wear multicolored spandex suits with capes in public. Now that would be embarrassing.

God, of course, is not a superhero. Though my stepsister once gave me a Jesus "action figure" that I keep on a shelf in my office right next to Nun-zilla, the fire-breathing nun. The packaging boasts "poseable arms & gliding action!" But God can't be contained inside the pages of a comic book. There are no God action figures available at Toys-R-Us. God's batteries can't run out. God can't be held hostage by those horrible plastic ties that come with superhero packaging. And God doesn't need expensive but critical accessories, like the Batmobile. But we can attribute some superhero-like qualities to God. God is on the side of good; God saves our souls, if not always the day; God never lets us down; God always prevails.

Grown-ups don't have all the answers about God; no human being does. But children seem to have all the questions. As a parent, I can only try to affirm the all-encompassing nature of God. When I'm asked if he will one day be taller than God, I tell Ben no. Since God is everywhere, that would be impossible. But to shrink God in Ben's imagination would be fair neither to Ben nor God. Occasionally, I feel that I'm getting through. When Ben looks up from his coloring book to tell me that the red Power Ranger is powerful but not as powerful as God, I claim a small victory. He understands that a force beyond his visible world exists and is at work.

In a child's world, so fraught with good guys and bad guys, I want Ben and Zack to know that God is good. Like Superman, God is on a neverending quest for truth and justice. At this stage justice, to the boys, is all about ridding Metropolis of evildoers like Lex Luthor. In time, I want them to discover that God is on the side of true justice, which is so elusive in our world.

Rummaging Around

Spring is tag sale season. Each weekend brings more bright yellow signs tacked to telephone poles as things old, new, borrowed, and blue are strewn across lawns and displayed in garages for all the world to see. And it's not just individuals holding these sales. It seems as if every institution holds a rummage sale—churches, schools, libraries, villages. Indeed, my own parish holds one every other year. For one full week we are inundated with rummage, culminating in a selling frenzy that raises close to $10,000 for outreach efforts.

What is it about rummage that always draws a crowd? For some, it's the amazing deals (a toaster for 50 cents!). For others, it's the thrill of the hunt. But for many of us, the opportunity to unload things is too much to pass up. Donating items to rummage sales gives us an excuse to clean out basements, garages, and attics. I live for the day when I'll be able to get to the back wall of my garage without tripping over unused sports equipment. When was the last time I actually used the lacrosse stick I played with in middle school? Yet there it sits, awaiting its chance to make me stumble.

There are several mysteries of the rummage phenomenon. First of all, where does all this stuff come from, and how did it get into my house? We aren't great pack rats, yet every year my family contributes bags and bags of stuff to the church rummage sale. Some of it makes sense—our boys have graduated from Bob the Builder to Power Rangers to Star Wars. And Bryna's pretty good about moving things along that we never use. Especially my stuff, like the dartboard that's been in the attic for a decade. Unbeknownst to me, she donated it to the church rummage sale last year. Somehow I refrained from buying it back. But other stuff just seems to appear. Who knew we had a fondue set we never used?

What makes the rummage cycle run, of course, is that someone out there wants a Bob the Builder Lego set or a dartboard or craves cheese fondue while rifling through used appliances. It's the rummage equivalent of the "Circle of Life" (speaking of which, we bought a copy of Disney's *Lion King* for $1). The truism that one man's trash is another man's treasure is never clearer than at a rummage sale.

It's embarrassing how many things we acquire over the course of time. Especially in light of the numbers of people in our midst, let alone the world, who have precious little. Perhaps giving things away assuages our guilt. But discarding our castoffs ignores the real issue, because this all leads us to a spiritual conundrum. At what point does physical baggage (i.e., all that stuff) become emotional baggage? Jesus is pretty clear on this: "Do not store up for yourselves treasures on earth, but store up for yourselves treasures in heaven. For where your treasure is, there your heart will be also" (Matthew 6:19). And while our initial thought makes us wonder how to "get" this treasure in heaven so we can horde it, we soon realize that's not the point. You won't find this treasure in the

"Antiques and Collectibles" room. For Christians, Jesus himself is that precious treasure. And if you place yourself in the hands of the divine rather than your things or even yourself, you will be rewarded. Salvation doesn't come through rummage.

This doesn't mean you must give away all of your possessions and decamp for the wilderness. Fortunately not everyone is called to this degree of sacrifice. I know I'm not. Not when I still fantasize about one day having a "man cave" in my house complete with a foosball table, big screen TV, leather furniture, and a bar. What it means is that we cannot allow our possessions to possess us. This is the inherent danger against which Jesus warns us. So it's not that things themselves are somehow evil. It's all about the priorities of our lives and how we relate to "earthly things."

I admit sorting through stuff to get rid of is cathartic. Bryna and a friend held a joint tag sale this year. They had a ball, and made a few hundred dollars between them. I think I scheduled a meeting for that morning. I just don't like the whole tag sale scene: the bargain hunters trying to haggle me down from ten cents to a nickel as if I owned a used-car dealership; people swarming all over my stuff, touching and then rejecting it; and the relentless efforts of our kids to buy back toys they haven't played with for three years.

But I do find the spring sorting that precedes a tag sale to be spiritually cleansing. And it's a lot cheaper than going to some New Age spa for a seaweed wrap. It's energizing to finally be able to walk outside in shorts and a T-shirt. Spring is literally in the air as I push the kids outside after a long winter of being trapped inside the house. And then it's down to the business of sorting and throwing out. The garage becomes my personal threshing floor as I separate the wheat from the chaff. Or in my case, the Goodwill pile from the tag sale stuff from the trash heap.

Coffee Talk

I never used to drink coffee. I made it through college, the army, work as a political campaign manager, a coffee-drinking wife, seminary, and one child. The combination of two children under the age of two and full-time work in parish ministry, however, put me over the edge. It's not as if I'm addicted now or anything. Really. I just can't imagine getting the day kickstarted without a steaming mug of coffee.

My Thursday morning sermon-writing ritual revolves around coffee. Or, more accurately, caffeine. Some church-goers need coffee to stay awake during the sermon. I need coffee to *write* the sermon. I'm not sure why this is, but I wouldn't want to subject anyone to the fruits of decaffeinated preaching preparation.

After searching for a couple of years, I finally found the perfect coffeehouse in which to write sermons. Coffee Labs in Tarrytown, New York, was founded in 2002, and I discovered it soon after. The name is actually a play on words. The logo incorporates an image of the owners' Labrador retriever, hence "Coffee *Labs.*" And since they roast their own beans (free trade, of course), it is also a coffee "*lab*oratory." The best part, aside from the coffee, is that it's a dog-friendly establishment. So Delilah and I head down to Coffee Labs every Thursday morning. I write, and she gets all sorts of attention. Everybody knows her name; I'm simply tolerated as Delilah's faithful companion.

One of the reasons I go out to write, besides the caffeine inspiration, is the need to get away from the distractions that hound me either at home or the office. I don't need perfect silence to write; I'm not a medieval monk working on an illuminated manuscript. I even welcome *some* distractions. The key for me is that they're not *my* distractions. So hearing the white noise of conversations or background music is fine. And I hardly even notice other people's children wreaking havoc around me (there's a great sign at the counter of Coffee Labs that reads: "Unattended children will be given a shot of espresso and a puppy"). As long as it is not *my* cell phone ringing or *my* children demanding my attention, all is well.

My one regret in being a java-come-lately is that I can't drink it black. Even Bryna makes fun of my "warm coffee ice cream." I admit I need the "fixin's" to fully enjoy the experience, even though adding cream and sugar makes me feel slightly less manly. What trucker stops in at the 76 Truck Stop in rural Mississippi and orders a light and sweet French vanilla?

But regardless of what kind of coffee you drink, there's nothing worse than getting grounds in your coffee. You look forward to taking that first sip and suddenly you've got small, black grains stuck to your tongue or lodged between your teeth. It's usually a problem with the filter. Perhaps it got folded over just slightly when you placed it in the coffeemaker. Easy enough to do in that pre-coffee morning haze.

But if a coffee filter strains out the grounds from our coffee, we need to do the same thing with life's distractions.

We need to filter out some of the incessant messages that bombard us and keep us separated from God's love. We have more control in this regard than we think, but it takes real discipline to self-filter our lives.

Often these distractions quietly weave themselves into our lives. They won't hurt us in the short-term—just as ingesting a few coffee grounds is more annoying than anything else—but they're things that continually distract us from keeping God at the center of our lives. Like becoming hostage to our e-mail or watching three hours of television before bed or never turning off our cell phones. These distractions can become like low-grade fevers; not debilitating but just enough to keep us from fully living. Things that don't require twelve-step programs but that, when abused, hinder our quality of life.

This past Lent I gave up checking my e-mail after 6:00 p.m. at home. It had gotten to the point where I could not disconnect, literally or figuratively, from the office. I know I'm not alone in this compulsion. People now refer to BlackBerrys—those handheld devices that allow you to check e-mail anywhere, anytime—as "Crackberrys." No one is so important that they need to check e-mail in bed.

Soccer Dad

Nothing screams "suburban dad" quite like standing on a soccer field on a Saturday afternoon. It's one thing to stand in front of a smoky grill with tongs at the ready or walk around the backyard with beads of sweat dripping from your forehead while wielding a weed whacker. But when you're staring at a bunch of kids swarming around a soccer ball on a weekend morning when you should still be in bed drinking coffee and reading the paper, you've reached suburban nirvana. You may as well take out a second mortgage on the house, because you're not going anywhere for a while.

It's fascinating to me how the most popular sport in the world binds American families together in a common weekend pursuit. At the appointed hour, thousands of cleated kids pour out of minivans all across the country. Parents, carrying travel mugs of coffee and those fold-up soccer mom chairs, trudge out behind them. This ritual continues every weekend during the fall and spring. At least until our kids graduate high school. Then no self-respecting American could care less about soccer. Which may be why the United States has never won the World Cup.

While most of us enjoy watching our children engage in athletic endeavors, it's amazing how many parents feel imprisoned by weekend youth sports. The constant shut-tling around to practices and games, the precious moments of free time being slowly sucked away by ten-minute quarters. No one's forcing you at gunpoint to sign your kid up, but guilt and suburban peer pressure are power-ful things.

I helped coach Ben's teams his first couple of seasons. It wasn't too much of a commitment at first—a brief Saturday morning practice followed by a half-hour game. But this eventually morphed into an hour-long Saturday practice followed by games on Sunday afternoon. Since I work on Sunday mornings (couldn't negotiate *that* out of my contract) and am pretty much spent by the afternoon, I just help out on an ad hoc basis when the coach needs an extra pair of hands. I particularly enjoy the pre-practice exercise where I'm the goalkeeper and all the kids take shots. At the same time.

Most coaches at the kindergarten level have little knowledge of the game of soccer. Their coaching careers began because *someone* had to do it. I actually love the game of soccer and in my glory days was captain of a lousy high school soccer team. But even if you import some Brazilian soccer star to coach your kid's AYSO squad, it still comes down to two basic concepts: kick the ball toward your opponent's goal and don't use your hands. That's as much coaching as a bunch of five-year-old boys and girls can digest. The nuances of the game are, shall we say, lost on this crowd.

Nonetheless, some coaches take this stuff pretty seri-ously. This despite the fact that no one's even keeping score at this level—"every game's a tie" is the mantra for these games. But not to some of these guys; they play to win even if no one else does. They probably call the parents the night before for bed checks just to make sure none of their players are out late partying. We played one team where the coach pulled out a dry-erase board between quarters to draw up plays. The kids dutifully gathered around to listen, but then when play resumed they swarmed around the ball like every other group of kindergartners in the free world. I'm sorry, but you're not Vince Lombardi; step away from the clipboard.

One thing I learned after awhile is that coaching your son doesn't work so well. Things I would tell Ben got either ignored or met with a look of complete annoyance. But when the same thing was said by a "real" coach, i.e., not his dad, he would respond immediately. As if my exhortation to throw the ball in to a teammate down the line instead of into the middle of the field was inherently flawed. But if Coach Ian said it, it must be brilliant strategy. I guess it's the same phenomenon you run into when you hear your child was so polite at a play date, saying "please" and "thank you." Are you sure we're talking about *my* kid? There are places where not being the parent is helpful to a child's development, and the soccer field is one of them.

In beginning youth soccer, as in life, it's helpful to keep things simple. When it comes to our faith lives, Jesus, too, urges simplicity. He distills everything down to the following: "Love God and love neighbor." Simple, straightforward, no frills. It's the equivalent of the two commandments of kindergarten soccer: kick the ball toward your opponent's goal and don't use your hands. When you remember the basics, everything else eventually falls into place. Even Pelé had to start with the basics, and it's not a bad place for us as well. We don't have to be fundamentalists to remember the "fundamentals" of faith. Love God and love neighbor. The fundamentals are what keep us spiritually grounded and focused. So if we work hard to love God and neighbor, we'll be in pretty good shape.

In the meantime, I'll see you on the soccer field. I'll be the one cursing the Good Humor truck that always seems to pull up just as the game is ending.

Multiple Choice

Too many choices can be overwhelming. I'm especially aware of this whenever I step into a diner. The menu goes on and on, page after page offering an amazing array of culinary choices. And I'm always a bit suspicious when I see so many items on a menu because there's no way any one restaurant can possibly do all of these things well. So I usually end up ordering the same thing, something I'm confident any diner can do well: I order the BLT.

This whole business of having too many choices was never clearer to me than when we renovated a kitchen a few years ago in Baltimore. Mind you, this wasn't a huge kitchen; we lived in a typical Baltimore rowhouse. But even so, the choices were mind-boggling: countertops, appliances, paint colors, faucets. And given our budget, this didn't include any of the myriad high-end choices, like which fancy chandelier to put in over the kitchen table (we didn't have one) or what color granite on the countertops (Formica's just fine, thank you). It would have been much easier if someone just held up several samples and said, "Here are five choices, pick one." But it wasn't that simple. I think I finally lost it when we got to cabinet knobs.

We spend a lot of time talking to the boys about making good choices. Inviting a lonely kid to join in your game of tag at the playground is a good choice. Teasing this same child for not having any friends is a bad choice. They're faced with such choices every day, and by highlighting these mini moral dilemmas we're just trying to get the boys to think ethically and realize that their choices impact those around them.

Zack often gets mad at me when I'm telling him to do something unreasonable like brush his teeth. "You're always the boss!" he screams. And, yes, I often am (unless Bryna's around). But I can see from his perspective how bossy I must seem: "Get dressed, eat breakfast, brush your teeth, put your shoes on, go to school." It must feel like I'm spewing an endless stream of commands.

As kids age, they gain more autonomy; they become "the boss" more often. And with this comes the responsibility of making increasingly important choices. Choosing between macaroni and cheese or a hot dog for dinner morphs into choosing a peer group, choosing to put in the extra effort on a science project, and choosing what college to attend (though the boys are still young enough that I've deluded myself into thinking they'll get athletic scholarships).

I've tried lately to point out the times when Zack is able to make choices and be in charge of certain things. Like what book he'd like me to read to him before bed or which direction he'd like me to toss him in the pool. He now realizes that sometimes he's the boss and at other times I'm the boss. And while he still gets annoyed that I get to be the boss more than he does, he also recognizes that I'm not *always* the boss. And it takes some of the sting out of my seemingly incessant bossiness.

When it comes to our faith lives, we, too, are offered a choice. Thankfully it's not as bewildering as trying to order at a diner or choose flooring for a new kitchen. The choice we're offered is to serve the one, true God or to serve any number of false gods, like money and control and power and human self-gratification. On the surface of things, it's a no-brainer. We'll just push the button to choose "God" and live happily ever after.

Of course, our faith lives are more complicated than a simple choice. Life is not a great multiple-choice test where we either choose the right answer and pass or choose the wrong answer and fail. The spiritual life isn't like *The Gong Show*. Each moment God grants us is an opportunity to again choose God, to put divine interests over human ones.

This isn't a choice we make once and for all, but one that we must make over and over again, each day, each moment.

There's a song in the animated version of the movie *Peter Pan* that the boys like to sing as they jump around the house with plastic swords. Captain Hook sings it as he's trying to recruit the Lost Boys to a life of piracy: "You'll love the life of a thief. You'll relish the life of a crook. There's barrels of fun enough for everyone! And you'll get treasures by the ton. So come and sign the book. Join up with Captain Hook!" But the chorus says, "The choice is up to you. Yo-ho, Yo-ho."

You do have a lot of control when it comes to making good choices in your life. As with the Lost Boys, the choice is up to you.

Dog Days

Bryna and I missed the whole online dating thing. When we were married, in 1995, eharmony.com was not even a gleam in the Internet's eye. I'm not complaining; I can't imagine a picture of someone in a clerical collar gets many hits. But I do feel like I made up for it recently.

That's because I finally caved in to the boys' incessant lobbying for a dog. Knowing next to nothing about pet adoption, we went where else? To the Internet. It turns out there are numerous pet adoption sites out there. So we narrowed our search to local shelters and rescue agencies and started "shopping." Hundreds of pictures of all sorts of dogs came up along with accompanying descriptions. So you'd see an angry-looking pit bull with the comment "not good with young children" or a cute little beagle with the observation "mostly housebroken." Never having experienced it, this is precisely how I imagine online dating works—pictures of people next to descriptions like "hates watching Monday Night Football" or "leaves the cap off the toothpaste."

This process of online doggy dating quickly became a family affair. The four of us gathered intently around the computer quickly judging the dogs by their covers, or fur in this case. And when we saw the one-year-old yellow lab/husky mix, we all knew this was the dog for us. After filling out an amazingly detailed application that included three references, we went to meet her and fell in love. She was gentle, sweet, and starved for attention. We found out from her handler that she was saved from a kill shelter in South Carolina—literally a "dead dog walking" until Pet Rescue stepped in to live up to its name.

The joke of this is that I'm really not a dog person. I grew up with cats, but since Bryna's allergic to them, she's always made it quite clear that it's either her or a cat. So when the ceaseless lobbying first started, I tried to be strong. I also knew I'd be the one destined to walk the dog in the pouring rain while Ben and Zack were at sleepovers, or doing homework, or off to college. And after all, we do have a goldfish. But as Ben pointed out, "You can't pet a fish, Dad." No, but they don't need to be walked, don't shed, and no one's ever been known to step in fish poop. This didn't fly.

Perhaps getting a dog was inevitable, but I still cling to my conspiracy theory: between Clifford, Scooby-Doo, and McDuff, parents are bombarded with images of cute, adorable, and crime-fighting dogs. Children's literature would have you believe that childhood without a dog is a form of parental abuse.

Of course, everyone in the family ignored my arguments and so Delilah has become the newest member of our family. Yes, I claimed naming rights. Assuming I'd be outside yelling her name for the entire neighborhood to hear, I refused Zack's suggestion of Chippy. I needed to retain some shred of dignity in this process.

In early October many Christian churches honor the little-known St. Fido. Officially we celebrate St. Francis Day on October 4, but in many parishes this is merely an excuse to bless pets. I'm not sure how St. Francis would feel about this, but he probably wouldn't mind. His concern for all God's creatures lends itself to the tradition. And it could be worse: at least his statues aren't buried upside down to facilitate a house sale, à la St. Joseph. Most pet blessings incorporate a wonderful blend of holy chaos—yelping dogs, skittish cats, hissing snakes. Precisely how I envision the hold on Noah's ark, except with vestments. St. Francis Day blessings provide profound testimony to the value we place upon the animals with whom we share our homes. And I was thrilled to be able to bring and bless Delilah the fall after we adopted her. We finally had a pet to bring! Transporting goldfish really doesn't work well.

But this is more than just a tale of suburban dog ownership. It's really a story of conversion (my own) and redemption (Delilah's). When we view our lives through the lens of the gospel, we tend to see God's hand most clearly. Considering the parables of Jesus are stories of everyday life, this is nothing new. Pets can open our eyes to the divine qualities of love and compassion. That's really why we bless our pets in October. But you don't need a pet to see that the human condition is full of encounters with death and resurrection, conversion and redemption. We just need to open our eyes to the surprising possibilities that surround us. There are lessons to be gleaned that transcend the superficial plane of our existence. They can be found everywhere—through our relationships (human, divine, and canine) and in the seemingly routine events of our lives. If a cat or a dog or even a snake can point the way toward harmony among us, what better way to honor the legacy of St. Francis?

We've come to love and cherish the newest member of our family, who's got me wrapped around her paw. She comes to the office with me, and she's become my faithful running partner. Of course, I also hear the words of the Prayer of Humble Access from the Book of Common Prayer in a new light: "We are not worthy so much as to gather up the crumbs under thy table." We'll just leave that to Delilah.

Win, Lose, or Draw

"Did you win?" Ben's question was disheartening. "No, but I finished" lacked flair. Running, and completing, my first race in seventeen years was a major accomplishment. Coming off the high of running a half-marathon after a long hiatus from competitive running was exhilarating. I was stumbling back into the house on sore and tired legs when I encountered Ben in the kitchen. And his question brought me right back down to reality.

I guess I shouldn't have been surprised. Because when success means Spiderman vanquishing the Green Goblin, merely "finishing" is uninspiring. That itself was the victory. Ben wasn't impressed.

Let's face it, no kid ever bragged, "My dad *finished* a race!" But life is about more than winning and losing. Nuance and moral victory are invisible to young children: I didn't win, therefore I lost. What I refused to lose, however, was the opportunity to engage my son in an important lesson of life and faith. Discussing the universal nature of competition transcends cliché. Because "Winning isn't everything, it's the only thing" and "It's not whether you win or lose, it's how you play the game" are incomplete. Winning is either overemphasized or undervalued. Which misses the point. What we learn about ourselves, the relationships that develop, and the way we treat one another are what matter.

This is rarely the message we send our children. No one remembers the horse that placed sixth in the Kentucky Derby. History forgets the man who lost the 1848 presidential election. Finishing 1,315th out of 2,020 entrants in a half-marathon is irrelevant. But when winning alone defines us, we regress to the five-year-old mindset. We are not ultimately defined by our jobs, our place in society, or even our bank accounts. Rather, we are defined by our relationship with God and the impact this has upon those whom we encounter. We are loved for the effort, whatever the result.

So whether we win or lose, falter or finish, God still loves us. Winning and losing can never define our self-worth. That's the beauty of relationship with the divine. And it's why this is such an important value for parents to impart to their children.

As a suburban kid, Ben's started to rack up some trophies. After each of his three soccer seasons, he's gotten a nice one. All the kids have. (I can't imagine how much athletic hardware teenage athletes must have—and where it all gets stored.) But I worry that my boys will start to *expect* awards just for participating. Life doesn't work this way. We want our kids to feel valued, but we also want them to strive to do their best regardless of what is or isn't at stake.

Perhaps I'm overanalyzing this. I admit I like getting medals. I got one recently for finishing the Chicago Marathon, and some of the other races and triathlons I've completed give them out after you cross the finish line. Usually it's just a T-shirt, but sometimes you get lucky (like if Nike is a sponsor) and they give out what are called "finishers' medals." I'm proud of the ones I have hanging on my wall and they make for good conversation starters. But I'd still run in races regardless of the "prizes."

That first race did lead to some great conversation between Ben and me. After the initial indignity, I explained that sometimes finishing is enough. There is joy in participating in something we love. Since Ben loves to draw, we looked at some of his artwork and I asked him why he likes art. He shrugged his shoulders. Art, like life, I explained, isn't about winning. It's about the joy of creating. For me, running is also not about winning—I'm not fast enough. But crossing the finish line is like finishing a drawing of which you're particularly proud. There's a sense of accomplishment and creation that exceeds the stark contrast between winning and losing. Ben stopped coloring his picture before it was complete and asked me to play Power Rangers with him. The conversation will continue.

God doesn't offer prizes for "Best Pray-er" or "Most Improved Spiritual Life." God simply wants us to be engaged in the relationship. This takes the pressure off and relieves our guilt over our imperfect faith lives. We don't have to "win" at the sport of devotion; we just need to occasionally take a step forward.

In time, I hope to run a race or two with my boys. I want them to experience the exhilaration of finishing. As a parent, I hope they win one or two of life's "races." Whether acceptance to the college of their choice or getting that promotion. But I also know that more often than not they will simply cross the finish line. And that itself is a winning effort.

The Wheels on the Bus

It happened again last week. In a hurry, late for an appointment, stuck behind a school bus. It's a late afternoon suburban hazard. The red lights start flashing, the stop signs slowly emerge, and the trail of cars grows longer, snaking behind the yellow bus like an exhaust-spewing cobra. There are few moments on residential roadways that render us so helpless. Sure, our highways get backed up during rush hour and there are days we seem to hit every red light. But the school bus slow-down is different. Our regular frenzied pace grinds to a halt the moment we innocently turn onto the bus route. And it drives me nuts.

I should know by now which streets to avoid at what times. But I don't. Diesel fumes must give me selective amnesia. So I sit and stew, flatly refusing to take a deep breath and count to ten.

We don't like being out of control and being stuck behind a school bus does just this. It places our carefully planned day at the mercy of the public education system. Our schedules literally take a backseat. But all aggravation aside, this is a wonderful metaphor for life and an important reminder about just who is in control. It's not us. As much as we'd like to order our lives to match our whims, it doesn't work that way. There is always a proverbial school bus idling between our desires and God's reality.

I'm not suggesting that God is a school bus driver, but I *am* saying that God operates on a timetable different from our own. And it can be frustrating. Things don't always go according to our own plans. So we end up waiting when we want to be moving. Or we end up moving before we're ready.

A few years ago I ended up with a stress fracture in my right hip. I spent two months on crutches, which made for awkward church processions. The doctor told me it was an "overuse" injury from too much running. Well, no kidding. Isn't that the point? At first I ignored the pain and tried to "run through it." No pain, no gain after all. But when it hurt even to walk, I gave in and saw the orthopedist, who shut me down effective immediately and gave me a pair of crutches.

I certainly didn't have time for this. It happened during the fall, the season in the church year when everything gets cranked up again. Moving in slow motion was not part of the plan. Simple tasks like getting the mail from the box across the street from the church became death-defying acts. I felt like the frog in the old video game "Frogger" trying to dodge cars and make it safely to the other side. Bryna suggested letting someone else get the mail, even if it meant waiting until the next day. What a concept.

A parishioner who recently had surgery gave me a bell to ring whenever I needed something from Bryna. She promptly put it on top of the refrigerator where I couldn't reach it. But the crutches themselves had their advantages. People often held the door for me in public places—nothing evokes more sympathy than a priest in a collar on crutches. And I loved my temporary handicapped parking tag. I despise malls, but it was worth going on occasion just to park in the prime spots right out front like a VIP while watching the other cars endlessly circle. Much to Bryna's annoyance I was fairly useless helping to put Zack and Ben to bed but, when necessary, I could squeeze the kids like chopsticks picking up a piece of sushi. Of course, they also delighted in moving my crutches just beyond arm's reach.

After quickly going through various stages of anger and frustration, I accepted my temporary nonambulatory state. It wasn't, after all, the end of the world. We can fume or get angry at our various predicaments, but it doesn't help. Just as we can rail against the unfairness of life. But the bus still stops at every single house in the neighborhood. The otherwise adorable ritual of parent meeting child takes place again and again, and you wind up later and later for that next meeting. But at a certain point, I usually become resigned to my fate. I take a deep breath and inch along, thankful for an unexpected moment of peace in my day. Annoyed, but thankful, if that's a possible pairing of emotions. Okay, mostly annoyed but at least trying to see the bigger picture.

Don't get me wrong; I understand school bus safety. I appreciate the drivers who wait patiently while Ben, Zack, and the other neighborhood children step aboard. My boys ride the bus every day, and I cherish the moments of father-son interaction waiting for the bus at the bottom of our driveway before I head to work. Usually the kids from across the street come over and we end up playing tag—I'm perpetually "it." Or, weather permitting, I get pelted with snowballs. I see other parents calmly sipping coffee while they wait for the bus. I'm not sure why my mornings at the bus stop are so active, though I probably bring it upon myself—it's too much fun getting the kids wound up and then sending them to the care of their teachers. Maybe it's my way of sticking it to the school district for getting stuck behind their school buses. And I've gotten used to showing up at my office winded and in need of fluids.

Wedding Bells

Emma and Zack have announced their engagement. Well, they haven't sent out the formal invitations and they have yet to register at Macy's. But according to both of them, they're getting married. I haven't been asked to perform the ceremony, but then again Emma is Roman Catholic so maybe they've already contacted another priest. That's fine. Doing the premarital counseling for your own child would be awkward. And what would I say about marriage to a couple of six-year-olds anyway? Fortunately, we like our future in-laws and Zack's brother-in-law to-be is one of Ben's best friends. So this should all work out nicely.

Whether they decide on a church wedding or elope in Las Vegas doesn't really concern me. What's exciting to watch from a parent's perspective is simply a growing level of intimacy among the boys' peers. Boy, girl, whatever, it's fun to see relationships blossom and flourish. And in Zack and Emma's case, there have been no reports of "playing doctor." Yet.

Friendship is one of the great blessings of this life. It's what adds texture to our very existence. And this is true whether you're hanging out on the playground in nursery school, eating French fries in some diner at 2:00 a.m. as a teenager, golfing with some buddies as an adult, or having lunch with a fellow widower. So observing your children begin to develop healthy friendships based upon respect and mutuality is a joy. Whether that translates into making mud pies or deciding to get married. Or both.

When kids are very young, they engage in what's called "parallel play." This means they basically play side-by-side; near each other but not *with* one another. This is one of those terms I'd never even heard of before I had kids. If asked, I would have guessed it was something the quarterback called in the huddle. But when you hang out around the sandbox enough at the local playground, you tend to pick up the lingo. Eventually kids move on to more interactive play and that's the spark of intimacy. All of a sudden they realize other people their size exist in the world and may even be worth playing with. At least until they have the audacity to touch their favorite Tonka truck.

As a sense of intimacy among children grows, the first sleepover becomes a rite of passage. So far Ben's had a few with his best friend Cole, but Zack's not yet ready to take this step. Unless you talk to Zack. Then you'd learn that Bryna and I are "mean and unfair." Naturally, Zack wants his first sleepover to be with a girl. It's perfectly innocent, obviously, but it makes me fear his teenage years even more. Next stop, the Elvis Chapel.

But a first sleepover is a big deal. And the idea of having to transfer a good portion of the entire bedtime routine to another location is daunting. Do you bring all eighteen of the stuffed animals? What about the nightly read-a-thon? And of course only *his* covers and pillow are acceptable.

Ben's first sleepover was traumatic—for us. *He* was fine. No separation anxiety to be worked out in future therapy sessions for this kid. But it was hard for me and

Bryna to fall asleep when you're expecting "The Call" to come in at any moment. You know, the one where you have to go out and pick up your child at midnight because he's too scared to fall asleep. Part of you is thrilled when the call doesn't come: "He's getting so grown up. He can sleep in a house without us." And part of you is depressed: "He's getting so grown up. He can sleep in a house without us."

The first sleepover is a tangible sign that we don't "own" our children. We know this intellectually, but the emotional piece is a bit harder to accept. They have our genes and our names and live in our homes, but they're God's children first and our children second. Even when they're young and utterly dependent upon us for their every need. But it's still difficult to accept that we are merely temporary stewards of our children and not their owners.

Soon enough they'll be off to college or moving out of the house for good (hopefully before they turn thirty). Like the security blanket they no longer need, they won't have to rely on us for everything. And that's wonderful. But it's also sad, if incomprehensible at this stage, to think about. Because as much as it drives me crazy when Zack leaps into our bed at 5:45 a.m. on a Saturday morning, yapping up a storm, all ready to start the day, I also love it. It means he still needs me in a very rudimentary way. And it's never clearer than when he starts yelling at me to go downstairs and fix him a bowl of Honey Nut Cheerios for breakfast. I assume he wouldn't make these demands on Emma's mom when he's old enough for his first sleepover, but who knows? I guess we'll find out in time. But not just yet. There's no hurry—Emma hasn't even picked out her wedding dress.

Class Mom

I'm the Assistant Class Mom for Ben's second-grade class.
The other class moms at the elementary school try to be
politically correct and refer to me as the Assistant Class
Parent. But I know my status, and I'm secure enough in
my "dadhood" to sign my e-mails "The ACM."

After nearly a year, I've determined the main thrust of
the job is to shake down other parents for cash: PTA dues,
teacher gifts, school fundraisers. I'm a glorified mob bag
man (or "mom" as the case may be). But at least they've
eliminated the phone chain. Before everything was com-
puterized, the primary duty of the Assistant Class Mom
was to organize those predawn phone calls on snow days.
Who wants to be known around town as the guy who
wakes people up with bad news?

But I didn't sign up for this position to be a novelty
act. I think it's important for kids to have male role mod-
els at school. Most of the class moms are, well, moms, and
nearly all the teachers are women. Yes, dads coach soccer
and baseball on the weekends, but I think it's also valuable for us to be present in our kids' academic lives. So
much of what we do for our kids is symbolic. When we
show up at their various activities and are involved in their
lives, they know we care. And such actions transcend
words. I tell Zack that I love him so often that when I say

this to him as I tuck him in, he'll sometimes look at me and say, "Yeah, yeah, everybody knows that." But I'll keep saying it, and I'll keep seeking ways to show this love through action and involvement. How could I *not* be an Assistant Class Mom? Plus I enjoy getting to know Ben's teachers and friends. As he gets older, this will be even more important as peer pressure kicks in—right now Ben *likes* me to show up in his classroom. I know the time's coming when he'll sullenly insist that I drop him off three blocks away from the school entrance.

There's also something about stepping out of our proscribed roles that's freeing. I still may be "Father Tim" when I go into the classroom, but primarily I'm Ben's dad. Or, as one child called me when he saw me in the hallway, "Dr. Phil." He knew I had some sort of title, he just couldn't place me out of context. Being the Assistant Class Mom also lets me gently break down some gender stereotypes while trying on a new role. We don't do this enough. Sure, you might get some odd looks at first, like when I showed up to the initial class mom meeting in the fall wearing a clerical collar. I assume most of it had to do with being a man. But in a school district that is overly sensitive to any display of religious symbols, I was a walking, talking one. Once the other moms got to know me and realized that I wasn't there to proselytize or run for the School Board, everything was fine. I don't need to make a statement by picketing for prayer in school. I'd rather make a statement about being a loving and involved father, father with a small "f."

And, yes, I was wearing my collar and Santa hat when I came to Ben's class in December to read *How the Grinch Stole Christmas*, but I somehow refrained from expounding on the Virgin birth. The tone was set when I walked in and one of Ben's classmates looked at me and asked in all sincerity, "Are you Hanukkah Harry?" Uh, no.

I may not be the best Assistant Class Mom at the boys' school. I'm horrible with anything having to do with crafts and I disappear during Holy Week and Easter. But the Class Mom is patient and understanding of my shortcomings, and I'm pretty sure that bringing the Dunkin Donuts "Box of Joe" on back-to-school night helped my cause.

Ghost Stories

Everything I know about exorcisms I learned from the movie *The Exorcist*. That classic 1973 horror flick had it all: priests gathered around the bed of a demon-possessed child while wearing black cassocks, holding up crucifixes, and mumbling in Latin. It was quite the scene.

I'm not a big fan of horror movies—I never understood why people would shell out good money to be terrified—but I do enjoy a good ghost story on occasion. Actually, it's been quite awhile since I've heard a ghost story. Maybe it's because I haven't been to summer camp for a few years now and the closest I've come to a campfire recently is firing up the gas grill in my backyard. And since Bryna's idea of camping is the Hilton, I'd have to take the boys camping alone. I might make it out alive, but I certainly wouldn't get any sleep.

But even though it's been a long time since I was last scared out of my wits at a campsite, sitting around and telling ghost stories is always memorable. There's something both comforting and disconcerting about it. You sit around in a circle, shoulder-to-shoulder with some close friends. There's a slight chill in the air from the late-evening summer breeze as the sun sets, and yet the warmth of the hot coals draws you in. You've had a hearty meal—maybe hot dogs and corn on the cob. Certainly something out of a can. And s'mores were undoubtedly on the menu. One or two marshmallows drop into the fire along the way, creating a fireball of gooey chemicals. Life is good. Then, as you gently let your guard down, there's a rustle in the woods. It's probably a chipmunk or a squirrel, but it *could* be a bear. And then someone begins to tell a ghost story. It starts out slowly and softly, barely audible above the crackling of the ever-dimming flame. The face of the storyteller glows in the dim light of the campfire. The tale builds to a crescendo and ends as the narrator suddenly leaps up to deliver the news that the creature is still alive and well and out to get you!

There are several stories in the Bible where the disciples mistake Jesus for a ghost. Not because he was particularly pale, but because his showing up made no sense. Like when he was seen walking on water. It must have been a ghost, they reasoned, because no one does *that*. And again when they encounter Jesus after the resurrection, the ghost theory is a perfectly reasonable conclusion. They just saw him die on a cross, yet there he was, in the flesh. Both are total Twilight Zone moments for the disciples, worthy of a call to Bill Murray and his Ghostbusters. Of course, unlike a classic ghost story, Jesus doesn't try to scare the unsuspecting disciples. He doesn't leap out from behind a tree wielding an axe. "Peace be with you," he says—hardly the chilling climax to a ghost story. There's a reason for this, of course. Jesus isn't a ghost and our faith isn't a ghost story.

We recently moved Ben's bed farther away from the window in his room. He was worried about someone coming in the middle of the night and "stealing" him. A bit irrational, of course, considering we have a security system, window locks, and bars on the window (he was a first child, what can I say?). But children's fears are very real, so we made a big production about moving his bed twelve inches farther from the window—there's only so much interior redesign you can do with such a small space. But Ben was satisfied and he *is* sleeping better these days. A testament to that fragile sense of security we all have, but only children seem able to admit.

Through his appearance to the disciples and through his presence in our own lives, Jesus exorcises the ghosts and demons of doubt and replaces them with faith. And Jesus also drives out a lot of demons from the possessed during his lifetime. These might make decent ghost stories—some of the demons are pretty scary, after all. I guess the church's equivalent of this is exorcism. I've never performed one, which is fine since I'd probably be woefully inadequate ("Oh, garlic is for vampires?").

I'm not even good at telling ghost stories. I can never remember precisely how they go and there's nothing worse than starting a story, getting people's attention, and then forgetting the point. I save this for the pulpit. It's just as well; the last thing I need to do is to scare the "bejesus" out of the boys right before bedtime. For now, I'll stick to reading them *Green Eggs and Ham.*

Jesus in the Mudroom

At our house the central loading and unloading zone is the mudroom, that small room just inside the backdoor where everything gets dumped. During the winter that means boots, snow pants, mittens, and jackets. During the summer that means flip-flops, wet towels, and the pool bag. When it's dry it means dirt; when it's raining it means mud, hence the name. I end up sweeping it on a regular basis because all sorts of muck winds up on the mudroom floor. Most houses have a similar space—whether it's a formal mudroom (there's an oxymoron for you) or just the spot where everything gets dropped when you come home. Dirt doesn't get intentionally shaken off in the mudroom; it just works out that way. And anyway, you'd prefer the dirt to end up on the mudroom floor rather than ground into the living room rug.

Our mudroom is very small, so when we're all leaving or coming in at the same time, it feels a bit like the running of the bulls at Pamplona. Except I get "gored" by flying shoes and doorknobs. The boys stampede through the mudroom with arms and legs flailing while the dog stands like a hurdle in the middle of everything. The mudroom seems to provoke a sense of great urgency to either get in or out of the house.

We all need transitional spaces in our lives. The mud-room is a transitional space between the outside and the inside. It eases the transition out into the elements, and it serves as a buffer between the exterior and the interior. I once watched an episode of a reality show where the father insisted on "transition time" after coming home from work. This involved sitting in a La-Z-Boy chair with his feet up drinking a beer and watching TV while mom raced around trying to get dinner ready, simultaneously dealing with three screaming kids. Eventually he got his due, which meant an end to his little routine. I hope he enjoyed it while it lasted.

I'm not going to hold this guy up as a model of enlightenment, but we all need some transition time in our lives. Parents with young children do need time and space to move in and out of the different roles: mom, employee, spouse. Much of this comes through negotiation. After a trying afternoon at home with the kids, Bryna may pawn them off on me while she goes out to do something glamorous, like groceries. You take alone time where you can. But after an intense day at work, I might want to go for a run to clear my head before jumping back into the domestic fray. It doesn't take a degree in marriage counseling to anticipate the marital train wreck waiting around the bend. We can't have it both ways, so we try to negotiate "transition time" with varying degrees of success. Often neither one of us gets a break. But simply recognizing that we all need it is important. At least you can identify the source of your crankiness even if you're still cranky.

For those who work outside the home, the daily com-mute may serve as the needed transition between work and family. That doesn't work for me, since the rectory is only a quarter mile from the church. You can't beat the commute (I figure it would take me three years to get through a Book-on-Tape Tom Clancy novel if I only listened on the way to and from church). But when I have "one of those days," I find it hard to disengage.

The mudroom at our house isn't just the place where we drop everything—though I wish I could get the boys to at least hang up their coats or pick up their baseball gloves. It's also the place from which we embark upon the day's activities. It's where shoes get put on and where umbrellas are kept. It's the jumping-off point for everything else. So sometimes I view it as our personal gateway to and from the chaos.

But in a metaphorical sense, Jesus himself is our mudroom. It is he who sends us out at the start of the day and it is to him we return at the end of the day. It is where we drop our emotional burdens and it is where we find the energy to move forward. We must pass through his presence each day to be equipped for the rigors of daily life. And we must return to his presence to be refreshed from the rigors of daily life. So the mudroom's not a bad place to be. It's a bit cramped sometimes—at least ours is when all four of us are trying to step over Delilah to get out the door at the same time. But it can also serve as a reminder that Jesus is with us at every step of the journey.

Too Cool at the (Town) Pool

We are drawn to it like lemmings to the cliff. The allure of the town pool is irresistible and, as temperatures rise, we just can't stay away. The post–Memorial Day routine begins slowly. But soon enough Bryna and I are struggling across the pool parking lot burdened down with towels, sunscreen, lawn chairs, snacks, and children, all in the hope of making it to the promised land of chlorine-soaked relief.

The town pool is our suburban oasis. And it's a wonderful phenomenon. One that has survived nearly unchanged over the generations. While bathing suit fashions and hairstyles have evolved and we now know the risks of sun exposure, the basics remain: hot sun, cool water, and lots of noisy children. But the town pool offers more than practical relief from the heat—you can go to any air-conditioned mall for that. For us, it's also a place of gathering and refreshment, conversation and laughter. The kids meet friends, we catch up with acquaintances, and life is good. And Bryna and I are slowly getting to the point where we'll actually be able to bring a book to read. I've always been a bit envious of parents of older children. They can read or carry on an actual conversation while their kids jump off the diving board for hours at a time without playing pseudo-lifeguard. But at least we're past the swim diaper stage.

The town pool is also one of the last truly intergenerational places in modern society. All of life's stages pass before me while I sit propped up in my chaise lounge. Elderly sunbathers with leathery skin, middle-aged dads sucking in their guts, young teenagers strutting their stuff, gleeful toddlers using kickboards, and screaming infants ready for naptime. These sights and sounds unite the childhoods of past and present generations. And it reminds us that as different as it is to grow up now, children remain children.

The only bane of my town pool existence, aside from the daily sunscreen wrestling match, is the snack bar. In our case, a kid magnet with mediocre food. No matter how much food we've hauled into the place, they still want $4 Push Pops. I'm sure I did too when I was their age, adjusted for inflation, of course, so perhaps it's all part of what makes the town pool the essence of summer childhood.

Besides the snack bar, it's a child plunging into the water with unencumbered joy, the unmistakable smell of chlorine mixed with sunscreen, a toddler trying to eat her ice-cream sandwich before it melts, teenage courtship on view for all to see, and the piercing sound of a lifeguard's whistle above the din. But it's more than just a summer playground. The gathered community transforms the town pool into a sacred place. The cool water provides a focal point for those who may have nothing more in common than geography.

In many ways the town pool is what the church should aspire to. It is a place of joyful abandon, all are welcome, and there's no litmus test required for entry. Except perhaps a bathing suit. Yes, there are some rules—no running, no horseplay—but they're all intended to maximize everyone's mutual enjoyment rather than to impose barriers between people. At the town pool, people sit around and gaze at the water because that's where the action is, just as in church people sit (or kneel) and gaze at the altar because that's where the action is.

There is also a wonderful universality at the town pool. No one looks out at the water and distinguishes between the Baptist swimmers and the Mormon divers. Pool water, like the sacramental water of baptism, is the great equalizer. And the town pool is a place where people are literally and figuratively stripped down to their basic humanity. The armor of high fashion is taken away; barring the use of a swim cap, expensive hairdos are washed away. In many ways this is precisely how God sees us: without our exterior defenses, without the fear-driven hyperbole that drives so many of our actions. God sees us stripped down to the core of who we really are. And it's freeing, if a bit frightening, to realize we are so well known. We are loved despite God's profound knowledge of our inner being. We are loved despite the fact that God knows our deepest desires and our innermost secrets.

The great challenge for me is getting the boys to come out of the pool when it's time to leave. I think every parent faces this same ordeal. While I can spend twenty or thirty minutes in the water, they could seemingly spend entire days in there. The words "Two more minutes, boys!" always bring them safely to the middle of the pool where I can't reach them. I may invent a water extraction device that would physically lift kids out of the water. Parents everywhere would be thrilled, and I'd make my millions and retire.

In time the days get shorter and Labor Day arrives. Soon enough we head back indoors. Back to our climate-controlled lives. Back to our over-scheduled existences. But for three glorious months, life at the town pool provides a wonderful respite from the impersonal nature of modern life.

I know a time will come when the boys will barely acknowledge my presence at the pool. They'll want to hang out with their buddies and my floppy hat will embarrass them. But for now I revel in roughhousing and playing monkey-in-the-middle with the boys and their friends. And I recall the times I spent swimming with my own father at another town pool in another place. The connections run deeper than the water. And I can't help but sit back in the sun and soak them all in.

On the Kitchen Floor

I often find myself on the kitchen floor. I'm not particularly clumsy. I just have two young boys who like to roughhouse and more often than not it starts in the kitchen. But after awhile Ben and Zack get bored and move on to other things. And I find myself sitting on the linoleum floor, staring at the dust bunnies under the refrigerator. I don't really mind the kitchen floor. It's hard to be full of yourself when your wife walks in and finds you stretched out on your back under the warm glow of fluorescent bulbs. It literally keeps me well grounded.

It was in one of these moments of prone reflection that I first noticed the chipped paint on the wall. It was just a small, insignificant patch near the baseboard. But I could see many layers of paint piled one on top of another. Which makes sense since it's an old house—built as a church rectory in 1883. The kitchen is currently painted white, but the chip revealed a number of previous color schemes, beginning with lime green, then yellow, olive, beige, off-white, red, and now white.

In my contemplative state, these paint chips reminded me of past generations. Not just the specific people who have lived in this house, but all those who have come before us in the faith. The span of life is not a snapshot. The present isn't the way things always were nor is it the way things always will be. There was a time before we walked the earth, and there will be a time when we walk the earth no longer. This isn't an earth-shattering revelation. But we so often live our lives blind to this reality. The kitchen floor isn't the only place I think about such things. I'm also aware of this anytime I sit inside an empty, historic church (I don't often find myself on *church* floors). But whenever I sit in a pew, I'm struck by the generations of prayers that have been said in these sacred spaces. Again, it keeps things in proper perspective. I'm not the only one who has ever wrestled with a particular spiritual issue or needed to lay a particular problem at the feet of our Lord. It's all been said before. And there's something comforting in this. It doesn't make our troubles or anxiety any less real, but it reminds us that we are part of something much larger than our individual situations.

And if I'm in a church with beautiful stained-glass windows, I can't help but think about those folks we call saints. They embody the past generations of the faithful—the paint chips of the Christian faith. But I also feel sorry for these misunderstood pillars of the church. Because people forget that the saints don't live just in these windows, frozen in the midst of the miraculous and immobilized in stained glass.

So it's helpful to broaden the definition of a saint to include all who have believed and died in the faith. Regular people. People you and I have known and loved and now miss—a father or brother, a friend, sister, or mother. People who have known Christ and touched our lives. Some saints are famous; others are long forgotten, painted over by subsequent waves of humanity. But all make up the vast communion of saints—the spiritual union between every Christian whether living or dead. Which is why a patch of chipped paint in an old rectory caught my imagination.

A famous passage from Ecclesiasticus begins, "Let us now praise famous men" and what follows is an ode to the famous men who were giants of their generations, "the pride of their times." But what's radical about this passage is what follows. Keep reading and you hear a eulogy to the forgotten and nameless people of faith. The ones no one remembers. They are the middle layers of paint; the greens and yellows and off-whites, the colors that have fallen out of favor over the years. The layers that have been painted over again and again and again.

So what about those forgotten saints? In a sense they're gone completely. It's as if they never existed. We can't remember anyone whose memory has effectively been wiped away forever. But the point is that it doesn't matter. Because God does not forget them. Their place of eternal glory is secure. Not because of what they did or didn't achieve during their lifetimes. But simply because of their faithfulness.

The current paint job in the rectory kitchen wouldn't be what it is today without the layers of the past. Even the forgotten layers. At one point, each old layer represented the new. At one point, they were all fresh coats of paint, gleaming and shining with fresh, up-to-date colors. At one point, they represented the present, not just the past. And so it is with us. We aren't the first generation to worship God, merely the present one. In time we will take our places behind new generations of present-day saints. We will be painted over but never forgotten by God. Our lives, our actions, even our paint colors will seem dated to future generations. But even if no one remembers us, God will. And there is great comfort in this.

Reflecting upon the layers of past, present, and yet-to-come keeps the immediacy of our own issues in perspective. Finding myself on the kitchen floor also keeps life in its proper perspective. As hard as it is to believe, life does not revolve around me. Which spending time on the kitchen floor makes abundantly clear. You can't be too taken with your own importance when your dog steps over you on her way to her bowl and throws you a glance that says, "You pathetic little man."

Portrait of the Artist

As an artist, Zack is nothing if not prolific. We literally go through reams of copy paper every year. He sits at the kitchen table with his bucket of markers yelling "More blank!" whenever he runs out of paper. I have a vision of him living as a temperamental *artiste* in a studio on the Rive Gauche in Paris. For now he colors all sorts of things: armed warfare, family portraits, cartoon characters, him dunking on me in basketball. The artistic onslaught never ceases. Which leaves us with the nagging question of what to do with it all. Some gets hung on the refrigerator, some gets sent to relatives, some makes its way to my office, but what about the rest of it?

We save the best ones in an album, but this only represents a tiny fraction of the total volume. If Zack only knew how much we stuck in the recycle bin, he'd be furious (I hope he never reads this). But Bryna and I are still wracked with guilt whenever we stealthily slip some of Zack's handiwork between the pages of yesterday's business section. And if he ends up as the next van Gogh (with both ears intact I hope), we're throwing away a gold mine. *Zack: The Early Years* could be worth millions.

We encounter a similar dilemma with Ben's schoolwork. He first started getting homework on a regular basis in second grade. With it, all sorts of projects and assignments and quizzes started making it home in his backpack. Again, what are parents supposed to do with all this stuff? We save a lot of it—probably too much—in a big box that sits in the attic. The rest, after cluttering up the kitchen for a week or so, goes into the garbage. At my worst I feel like I'm pitching his childhood onto the trash heap. But what are we supposed to do with an old math test on which Ben got an 85 percent? Is that memorabilia? And if I saved every scrap of paper with his name on it, what would he do with it when he's my age? Chances are, he'd toss it himself. So I'm eliminating the middleman, or that's what I tell myself.

Mostly I want to keep all of Zack's art or Ben's schoolwork because I want to remember them at this stage of life. I want to remember their accomplishments along with their frustrations (those are the crumpled-up pieces of paper from Zack's perfectionist stage). But of course I can't keep everything just as I won't be able to remember everything. I've already forgotten all sorts of cute things they've said that I should have written down. Although if we spent all our time transcribing our children's lives, chances are we'd miss a lot. It reminds me of those tourists you see who spend their entire vacations looking through the lenses of their video cameras. Sure, they have some great images from the trip, but how much of it did they really experience?

I admit I was a pack rat as a kid. I saved everything: old report cards, term papers, every single letter ever sent to me, Cub Scout badges, not just the baseball cards but the *wrapper*s they came in. Over the years I've weeded everything down to three boxes in the attic. Well, that doesn't include the boxes and boxes of baseball cards, but those live quietly underneath the bed, so they don't count. Out of Bryna's sight, out of Bryna's mind. So what made me finally see the light on the rest of my stuff? When my mother gave it all to me after I graduated from college and said, "Here, *you* haul this around the country for the rest of your life." Ouch.

I'm not sure why I feel so compelled to hold on to the things I've kept—my three boxes' worth. I have various items with which I just can't part. Like Little League team photos, letters from close friends and family (I did pitch the ones from old girlfriends), a few LPs, a bunch of photographs. I guess this stuff is comforting because it represents a part of who I am, or at least a piece of who I was. It's nostalgia, a link to the past, a tangible way of marking my existence in this fleeting and fragile world.

Yes, Jesus tells us not to store up for ourselves treasure on earth but rather to seek treasure in heaven. And we all do our best. A few mementos can't hurt, as long as we're not trying to live exclusively in the past. We should be okay as long as we remember that it's not the things themselves that define us but rather our relationship with God.

But it's a fine line. Because as insecure human beings, we often fret about our legacies and speak about wanting to "leave our mark." We want our names to live on forever so that people won't forget us when we die. Over the years this idea has caused many to go to extreme measures to secure enduring legacies. In Egypt the kings built massive pyramids. Louis XIV built Versailles. Donald Trump built Trump Tower, among other monuments to himself. And it's why people build those huge mausoleums you see in cemeteries. While the building materials may differ, the principle remains the same: build something that will endure throughout the ages and you will never be forgotten.

But it doesn't work that way. The realm of the eternal is God's alone. Fortunately, God never forgets us. So even if my three boxes get lost in the next move, it's not the end of the world. And even if I don't save every sheet of Zack's artwork, the world will survive.

Tooth Decay

Four cavities. That was the report from Ben's dentist after our last visit. I was shocked. While we're not the best at reminding the boys to brush after breakfast, it's not like they subsist on Bit-o'-Honey and Pepsi. They generally eat balanced meals and, yes, I realize that dinosaur fruit snacks don't count as fruit. So I took Ben's tooth decay as a personal affront to my parenting skills. It was probably just my imagination, but I swear the dental hygienist was giving me dirty looks, as if she'd caught me pumping Ben with Twinkies and withholding fluoride as a form of abuse. Next time I'll feed him a box of Oreos before I send him to get his teeth cleaned.

Actually, I had lousy baby teeth myself, and poor Ben seems to have inherited this. As a result, a trip to the dentist still sends chills down my spine even though I haven't had a cavity in over twenty-five years. It all feels like a trip to some medieval torture chamber. They stick the suction tube halfway down your throat until you start gagging and then they gleefully start scraping away with that miniature meat hook. All while talking at you incessantly as if you're in a position to communicate. Of course, it's that horrible whirring of a dentist's drill that is the stuff of nightmares. With all the technological advances we've seen, why can't they invent a silent drill? Or at least one that makes a different sound. My theory? Dentists like it.

I don't mean to be too hard on dentists; theirs is an important if unpopular job. When I was growing up, we had a dentist who lived in the neighborhood. You only had to stop by his house once on a Halloween night to realize it wasn't worth the effort. Instead of Snickers bars or Mary Janes, he gave out toothbrushes. Way to be a wet blanket on what was otherwise the best night of the year.

In one of my many trips to the electric, I mean dentist's, chair as a kid, I told the dentist not to use Novocain. I didn't want the shot into my gums, and I figured that without it I'd avoid that annoying numb feeling in my mouth for the rest of the day. The dentist was remarkably agreeable and enthusiastically whipped out his drill. It took one pass over the cavity before I broke down in agony. I don't think I've ever experienced such pain in my whole life.

Part of my struggle with Ben's four cavities is that I don't want him to experience pain. I know that's irrational—pain is part of life. But protection is a natural instinct of any parent. We want to shield our children from physical and emotional pain. When we can't, it hurts and it exposes our limitations as parents. I can't ultimately protect his teeth anymore than I can protect him from having his arm or his heart broken in high school. Emotional and physical pain is an integral part of the human condition. As an adult you understand this; as a child you must learn this.

No one ever guaranteed us a pain-free existence. All you need to do is look at the cross of Christ for proof of that. We're promised lots of things—relationship with

God, eternal life, the fruit of the Spirit. But there's no assurance that we won't, at times, experience heartache and grief. That's really what I want to protect Ben from—the cavities are merely a physical extension of the desire to protect him from life's pain.

I don't need to moralize about the violent images kids are exposed to through movies, cartoons, and video games. I watched hours of Road Runner cartoons and lived to tell about it. When I show concern for the villain being pummeled by Batman, the boys both glare at me with an exasperated expression and say, "It's not real, Dad." So they're better able to distinguish between virtual and actual pain than I give them credit for. Still, becoming desensitized to onscreen violence differs from feeling real pain.

When Ben was five, he had surgery to close an open hernia in his belly button. It's fairly routine stuff—it's an outpatient procedure. But they did have to put him under, and it took a few days of uncomfortable recovery at home. Ben did wonderfully, but the hardest part for me and Bryna was watching him go under with the anesthesia. It's disconcerting to see your vibrant and energetic little boy's body suddenly go limp. But Ben did learn about physical pain beyond scraping a knee. He also tried to milk the attention and extra special treatment well after the pain wore off. That's when we knew he was fully healed.

I assume Ben's adult teeth will come in stronger than his baby teeth. Perhaps advances in pediatric dentistry will keep him out of the realm of dentist chair phobia. In the meantime I have a feeling that getting him to go back to the dentist will be like, well, pulling teeth.

Snow Day

The dreaded call usually comes at about 5:00 a.m. It confirms what we suspected when we went to bed: snow day. Even in my sleep-induced stupor, I make sure to pick up the phone on the first ring. If the call wakes up the kids, they'll want to go sledding immediately. Who cares if it's still dark, with sub-Nordic temperatures and blizzardlike conditions?

No single issue in our house so divides kids and parents. The boys are thrilled with a snow day. And from a kid's perspective, what's not to like? For one thing, it means the previous night's "snow dance" worked. Plus they don't have to "do" anything on a snow day besides pelt me with snowballs, go sledding, build snow forts and snowmen, make snow angels, and end the outing with steaming mugs of whipped cream–topped hot chocolate. This so beats the alternative of sitting in school at circle time and listening to the teacher read *Harold and the Purple Crayon*. Even though that sounds great to me.

Then there are the adults, whose response is slightly more restrained than the boys' unbridled joy. After the kids wake up, find out there's no school, and start jumping on our bed, Bryna and I begin the day by canceling our various meetings. But the major difference between the two responses is that when it comes to snow, the boys play in it and we're left to shovel it and drive in it. It never used to be this way. One of the clearest signs of aging is that I do the "anti-snow dance" to try and offset the boys' efforts.

The heightened sense of joy in a snow day stems from the fact that children seem hardwired to hate school. Even though they love going to school to see their friends, even though they take pleasure in all the activities, and even though they secretly adore their teachers, if you ask them how they like school they respond immediately with "I hate it." At least that's the case in our family. This takes tangible form in the daily struggle to get the kids dressed and out to the bus stop. "Why don't you want to get dressed?" "I hate school." "What are talking about? You had a great time yesterday." "I hate school."

We're fortunate to have a pretty steep hill on the rectory property that's perfect for sledding. But before we can even think about sledding, we first must don the cold-weather battle gear. If it's the first snow of the year, we spend twenty minutes hunting for snow pants in the attic. Finally we find them in the box with the Christmas ornaments. Then we spend the next fifteen minutes looking for boots. Oh, they were in the front hall closet where they belong. Who knew? Then comes the layering process that turns the boys into the Michelin brothers. And, finally, without fail, comes the "Dad, I have to go potty." Of course you do, even though I asked you about this five times before getting you dressed. At least we get to avoid the fight over sunscreen.

Eventually we get outside. Snow has the same effect as a swimming pool—the boys could stay in it for hours, long after any normal adult could stand it anymore. If I stayed outside as long as Ben and Zack, they'd have to amputate several of my digits due to frostbite. But getting outside makes it all worthwhile. The boys have a blast racing down the hill. My job, like a beast of burden, is to haul the sled back up the hill after each run. It's generally a thankless job, but I barter a few runs of my own—it's still a great adrenaline rush and the boys take an oddly intense pleasure in watching me wipe out.

Once I get beyond my initial annoyance at having my schedule turned upside down, I can appreciate the value of a snow day. It's a forced Sabbath. And since most of us are lousy at planning days of intentional rest into our lives, it's good to let God whitewash our calendars sometimes. We're not as important as we think we are. Amazingly enough, life goes on even if we have to cancel a meeting or two.

Sabbath is a big concept in religious circles. Spiritual writers are forever extolling the virtue of spending a quiet day in reflection and prayer every week. It sounds great, of course, but they obviously don't have young kids at home. Or a spouse. "Bryna, I'm going off to walk in the woods for the next eight hours. Have fun with the boys." It's just not happening. Maybe when the kids are old enough for sleep-away camp, I'll be able to piece together more than an hour or two. But it may have to wait until we're empty nesters; or at least for that brief interval before they move back in with mom and dad after college. But in this season of life, you take what you can get. Besides, the woods get awfully cold in the dead of winter.

Road Trip

Driving a minivan is not cool. I've tried everything to enhance my image while behind the wheel, but nothing works. Sleek sunglasses, blasting Led Zeppelin on the stereo, peeling out. No matter what I do, I still look more like a soccer mom than a NASCAR dad.

For many auto enthusiasts, you are what you drive. So tooling around town in a muscle car or a BMW or a pickup truck is an extension of your personality. I don't fully buy this, but what I drive is certainly an extension of my stage in life. And I can just imagine the look Bryna would shoot me if I announced I was getting myself a sporty new two-seater. It's not happening. But fifteen years from now? Look out.

My first car was a bright red 1980 Volkswagen Rabbit. Now, that was a thing of beauty. A souped-up, four-speed stick shift with black vinyl seats and no air conditioning. Climate control meant rolling down all the windows and driving fast. My friends and I would cram into that thing like clowns at a circus and speed all over the place. If your first car is the ultimate symbol of freedom, the minivan is the ultimate symbol of domestic imprisonment. "Fully loaded" used to mean a sunroof, AC, and a hot stereo; now it means sixteen cup holders and a DVD player. And, let's face it, you can't go out cruising in a

Honda Odyssey. Well, you could, but it would be called driving the car pool.

Despite all the technological advances, families still do take long car trips during summer vacations. This remains a staple of the American experience, whether it's to the Grand Canyon, or Grandma's house, or just because you view sitting in traffic on the New Jersey Turnpike as quality family time.

The biggest difference between road trips as a kid and a road trip *with* kids is the whole safety thing. My brother and I used to stretch out in the back of the sedan with nary a seatbelt, booster seat, or side-impact air bag to be found. The only road rage we encountered was the result of Matt having the nerve to place a finger on my side of the backseat. Now the kids are strapped into their car seats, immobilized. And instead of playing the license plate game, they're watching *Shrek* until their eyes glaze over. Distances aren't measured in miles but in movies. "Buckle up, boys, this is a three movie trip."

In those brief unplugged moments along the way, car travel lends itself to conversation. A long car ride is the perfect opportunity to catch up with a spouse or a child. Parents of teenagers tell me the car is the perfect place to have important talks with their kids. Mostly because they're trapped. And when I'm not refereeing disputes and threatening to "turn this car right around," family trips are great opportunities for quality time with our boys.

One positive change in family travel is the advent of the E-ZPass. When we lived in Baltimore and Bryna's family lived in New York, we regularly traveled up there for visits and spent plenty of time in toll lines. We had the added challenge of an infant son who invariably woke up from a nap whenever the car stopped. After a few trips we decided to investigate the then new E-ZPass system that allows cars to zip right through tolls. What a difference! I admit that I felt special driving past long toll lines, like I had some secret VIP privileges. I might have felt slightly guilty the first time, but I got over it pretty quickly. And since Bryna dealt with the bill whenever it arrived, it was like all the tolls were suddenly free.

Approaching God is a bit like having E-ZPass. God is always inviting, always encouraging us into a deeper relationship. And God always gives us access to this relationship through prayer, through Scripture, and through faith in Jesus. True, we often create our own "tollbooths" that keep us from the love of God. But, much like actual tollbooths, they are merely human structures. If we allow God more fully into our lives, these tollbooths can be wiped away and the road toward God opened once again.

I admit that a minivan does make long car trips more comfortable. Everyone has room to spread out even though whoever's in the passenger seat has to act like a contortionist whenever the kids demand snacks in between movie showings. Maybe I'll look into putting racing stripes on the sides.

Cable Guy

I don't live on the edge. Certainly not on the cutting edge of technology. For one thing, we just got cable TV. Not HD, not satellite, not DirecTV. I'm talking basic cable here. I think we may have been the last holdout in metropolitan New York. We still don't have HBO, so any parishioners dying for a reference to *The Sopranos* in the Sunday sermon will leave disappointed.

Why didn't I want cable? Well, I'm cheap. But besides that, I'm morally opposed to paying for television. Isn't that why we're subjected to so many commercials? And don't talk to me about TiVo—I don't even know where it comes from or how to use it, let alone how it became a verb. I also theorized that if I had cable I'd want to get my money's worth every month, which might translate into watching eight straight hours of *Law & Order* reruns in the waning days of November.

My resistance to cable went beyond the money angle. As a parent, I had a deep-seated fear that could be summed up in three words: the Cartoon Network. Cartoons twenty-four hours a day? Are you kidding me? If that existed when I was a kid, I'm pretty sure I would have *become* a member of the Jetson family. Talk about turning the boys' young, formative minds to mush over a single billing period. I don't mind Ben and Zack watching some

TV—I gave up the naïve notion of shielding them from the television monster the moment I plopped Ben in front of a Baby Einstein video to get a moment of peace when he was an infant. But *SpongeBob SquarePants* has literally not one shred of a redeeming quality. I know; I've watched a bunch of the hypnotic episodes with the kids.

In some ways, the decision to get cable came down to the reception thing. We barely got any. Despite my most creative efforts using rabbit ears and tin foil, some nights our television functioned as little more than an oversized radio. Bryna just couldn't take it anymore, and she didn't buy my argument that seeing two Jerrys on *Seinfeld* reruns made the show even funnier.

How'd we finally end up with cable? Not surprisingly, Bryna subverted my flimsy authority in a creative way. She got me cable for Christmas. She gave me some line about wanting me to be able to see sports more clearly, but when she's hogging the remote to watch HGTV, I have my doubts. And of course when the cable bill comes every month, it becomes the ultimate gift that keeps on giving.

One show we watched recently was the *Super Nanny*. I can't remember if it was on cable or network television, but since it's all about dysfunctional family life, it was finally a reality show to which I could relate. As opposed to being stuck on a tropical island trying to "survive" or facing Donald Trump in the boardroom. If you've never seen it, there's a woman known as the Super Nanny (British, of course) who steps in and sorts out extremely disordered family situations. Like a superhero of codependence, she swoops in to save the chaotic day. It's not one of my favorite shows, because after we finally wrestle the kids to bed and can relax for a few moments the last thing I want to do is watch *other* parents try to get *their* kids to bed.

I also get to watch television preachers. Most of the theology's pretty lousy, but some of them are entertaining in an I-want-to-avert-my-eyes-but-it's-hard-not-to-look kind of way. Some are slick, some are passionate, some are scary. But they all have 900 numbers and bad hair. I know God works through a variety of people in various ways. But must they all take Visa?

Maybe part of me is jealous. These guys always seem to fill huge auditoriums and people hang on their every charismatic word. They reach thousands of people through their television ministries. I'm lucky to get one hundred people on a Sunday morning, and I know at least a few of them are reading the announcements in the bulletin during the sermon. When I preach I rarely move people to the point where they fall on the ground and writhe around in spiritual ecstasy. Okay, that's never happened. But I also know I'd make a terrible televangelist. Most of my suits are made of natural fibers, Bryna doesn't wear nearly enough makeup, and I believe theology is much more nuanced than the black-and-white, made-for-television preaching that rules the airwaves. Though I do wonder what I'd look like in High Definition.

At this point I could never go back to life without cable. It's nice to be able to see the baseball when I watch my Orioles lose to the Yankees. And it's nice to be able to find something to watch when Bryna and I want to relax after the kids have finally gone to sleep. Who knew that news anchors actually had facial features? But I feel good about having made it nearly forty years without cable. It's a cheap and literally fuzzy moral victory. But I'll take it.

Back to School

That horrid grinding sound you hear the week after Labor Day is the wheels of the regular schedule starting up again. At our house we seem to get more and more lax as the summer goes on. Who cares if Zack wears his PJs all day? The cashier at the grocery store doesn't seem to mind. Or if Ben watches three straight hours of cartoons before breakfast? Isn't that the point of summer vacation? We let the kids stay up later at night in hopes that they'll sleep later. It's one of the mysteries of the universe that this never correlates.

The trouble with our vacation mode starts when the lazy days of summer run smack into the regular routine of the other nine months. In an instant we transform from a houseful of slugs into the morning routine of Marine boot camp. Some parents try sleep training for a week or two before school starts. They ease their kids back into the routine by getting them to bed at a more reasonable hour and waking them up earlier. By the time the first day of school rolls around, the theory goes, they'll be leaping out of bed to greet the school bus. Even if we could remember to try this earlier than the night before the first day of school, I still don't think it would work very well on D-Day. Behind all the nice pictures we take as the kids step onto the bus for their first day of whatever new grade they're entering lay arguments and threats and cajoling and bribes. Once they're outside everything's fine; getting them to that point is mind-numbing.

That horrid grinding sound I mentioned becomes that horrid whining sound on the first day of school. And all the sleep training in the world wouldn't change that. Because backpacks and lunches and school clothes and homework and new teachers aren't nearly as engaging as watching six straight hours of *Teen Titans*.

At the root of the protests, of course, is anxiety. Kids aren't going to wax eloquent about the difficulty of change and transition. They whine. And starting a new school year is fraught with anxiety. For parents, this translates into the inconvenience of whiny kids; for your children, the first day of school can be an experience bordering on the traumatic. Sure they adapt quickly, but it's nerve-racking to be put in a new environment with new teachers and new classmates. When we minimize their stress, we're not being fair to them.

One of the rights of passage this time of year is doing the back-to-school shopping—for some reason I always liked picking out new school supplies. We'd always go right before school started, and there was that anxious excitement in the air. I still get a thrill whenever I wander through a Staples. I'm not sure why, since I couldn't care less about office products. I'm neither a file folder junkie nor am I obsessed with paper clips. Maybe it's that hypnotic smell of new office supplies that leads you to believe you really need another Rolodex. Okay, it's the shredder that I covet. I have no top-secret documents to destroy lying around my office; I just like the idea of shredding stuff.

Ben and Zack hate shopping for school supplies. At least that's what Bryna tells me; she mercifully takes them to Target every year. But I think I know why they despise these excursions. They've moved the back-to-school sales so early that they just serve as a midsummer reminder that vacation doesn't last forever. If you try shopping for the ever-popular Trapper Keeper after Labor Day, you'd never find one—they're all sold out by then. My other theory is that my sons genuinely just don't care about office supplies.

Whether it's getting back to the regular routine after a vacation or going back to school, transition is difficult for everyone. God is well aware of this, which may be why we're even more attuned to the divine presence when things change. The loss of a loved one, a cross-country move, being downsized from a job, making a midlife career change, even having a child—these are all dramatic changes from the ordinary. Adults aren't given the luxury of being able to whine in public, but turning to God amid all the changes inherent in this life allow us to focus on the one rock of stability that endures through it all. And that's a source of both strength and comfort.

It's tough for everybody to make transitions. I find it particularly difficult to shift from vacation mode back to real life. Going directly from the beach to the office is no fun, and it always takes me awhile to adjust. Though I've also found that counseling someone while wearing a bathing suit and reeking of cocoa butter is inappropriate.

Thank-You Note

Being a parent is a thankless job. Not because it isn't rewarding, but because our kids never actually thank us for all our efforts. Maybe they do in some speech at the rehearsal dinner the night before their wedding, but that's a lifetime away. At this stage, I'm not expecting one of them to say, "Dad, thank you so much for taking away my play date with Cole. You're right; I should have done my homework without a fight. Thank you for teaching me that valuable lesson about responsibility." Instead, this is translated as "Dad, you're so mean; I hate you."

There are other ways we get thanked, of course. I remember coming home after a particularly contentious meeting at church to a note Zack had written, with some spelling help, that said, "Dad—You're Awesome." I'm not sure where or why the inspiration arose, but it was exactly what I needed to hear. By the time I found it, he had moved on and was yelling at me to fix the dead batteries in his remote-controlled car, but the point had been made.

When I was a kid, I hated writing thank-you notes. It didn't exactly take the joy out of getting presents, but the dreaded thank-you note always loomed over any celebration. Before the wrapping paper had even hit the floor, it seemed my mother was nagging me to start writing them. And my procrastination gave her good reason to nag. But there's nothing worse than being dragged away from a new toy and plopped in front of a blank note card. Yes, I was thankful for the gift. But knowing it would inevitably culminate in the obligatory thank-you note was a downer. Especially when the gift itself was hardly worth the agony. A new football, fine. But it's hard to sound enthusiastic about that "fantastic new pair of socks you sent me for my birthday! Thank you so much!" And somehow my mother never bought my argument that if I just waited until after Christmas, I could save postage by sending *one* note to thank Aunt Wanda for *two* gifts.

As a parent I now do the same thing to my kids. "Happy birthday! Now start cranking out those thank-you notes." And given their reaction, you'd have thought I'd asked them to remove their own tonsils. With Zack, I'm simply asking him to write his name. I've already done the hard part: I found the note card, addressed the envelope, and wrote the note to thank Henry for the pirate costume. Okay, who am I kidding; Bryna actually did all this. But still, it takes weeks of Cold War–style negotiating to get them all done.

If you did anything else in your life that was as thankless as parenting, you'd quit. If it was a volunteer committee, you'd stop attending meetings. If it was a job, you'd pull out the help-wanted ads. But parenting is different. No one becomes a parent for the regular affirmation. One day of parenting cures that notion. It is deeply rewarding and satisfying and affirming in many ways—it just doesn't usually take the form of a traditional "thank you" from the objects of our love and concern and anxiety and frustration and responsibility. But it's okay, because there's always a hug or a high five or some other glimpse of gratitude that sustains us.

I've always found it intriguing that we need a national day of Thanksgiving to remind ourselves to pause and give thanks. Granted it's become more about the "three Fs"—food, family, and football—than anything else. And it's possible that our thanks might be misdirected—perhaps it goes to Aunt Helen for not burning the turkey this year or to ourselves for setting the table with such perfection. Or to Granddad for refraining from his unbearably distasteful political commentary. But the little secret about Thanksgiving Day is that the thanks actually goes to God. That's why the Pilgrims first gathered, not to watch huge men chase a pigskin on a television screen in order to avoid members of their extended family. (Sorry, was I projecting?) And as much as God desires our thankfulness, God doesn't nag us or withhold love for us. Thankfulness isn't a requirement or a prerequisite to God's grace. But a lack of gratitude can be a stumbling block in our relationship with God.

One of the most common phrases spoken by parents of young children is, "Don't forget to say thank you." I say this countless times a week because, well, they forget to say thank you. Whenever I go to pick up one of the boys after a play date, there's that requisite moment as they put on their shoes to leave. "What do you say?" I ask. "Thank you," they mutter. Other parents tell me my boys are very polite. Really? I guess they save it for moments when I'm nowhere in sight. But saying "thank you" goes beyond good manners. And hopefully one day, aside from learning to say "thank you" without being asked, they'll see that the source of all thankfulness is God.

Germ Warfare

I'm not overly sensitive about dirt. If one of the boys drops a hotdog at an outdoor barbecue, I'll just brush it off and let them keep eating. If people are looking at me, I might make more of a fuss over cleaning it off. But I'm not throwing it out. Five-second rule? More like five minutes. There's some statistic floating around about how much dirt the average person consumes in a given year. It's something like five pounds worth. So what's a few extra ounces of dirt from a dropped chicken nugget?

It's not that I'm reckless about this stuff. I make the boys wash their hands before dinner if I remember, but if cleanliness is next to godliness, then I'm a lousy parent. I'm proud that Ben and Zack look like actual kids. They may sometimes come inside with dirt streaked across their faces or chocolate milk stains on their chins, but that's why God invented the washcloth. No one will accuse them of being Stepford children—you've seen kids who never have a hair out of place, always wear clothes from Talbots, only speak when spoken to, evidently never spill food, and never, ever act up in church. They're clearly aliens.

Kids are basically dirty by nature. At least boys are. Some parents never want their kids playing in dirt. "Don't get dirty!" they scream. Well, at some level it's what they do for a living. But I agree there's a time and a place for it. Making mud pies just before going to Grandma's for Easter dinner isn't one of them.

After a particularly bad downpour of sleet and freezing rain, I remember looking out the window and watching the boys making "mud angels" in the backyard. In their new winter coats. And it made me cringe. A lot of our negative reaction comes from the fact that, as adults, we'd never do this. It's gross! But sometimes, as parents, we need to set aside our own feelings and let kids learn for themselves how things feel. Whether that's jumping into a puddle or playing with wet leaves or making mud angels.

The only time I get a bit compulsive about hand washing is after a visit to the pediatrician's office. No matter how upscale the practice, the waiting room is always crawling with germs. You can practically see them on the Tonka trucks. That canister where they keep the Legos is basically a germ bucket. Snot-nosed toddlers grab them by the fistful. If the kids weren't sick when they came in, they'll certainly catch something while they're waiting to be seen. Not a bad scam from the doctor's perspective.

We naturally want our children to be safe and secure, but we can't coat them in bubble wrap. Dirt and even germs are facts of life. Advertisers have created a culture of fear where a modicum of caution would suffice. And those commercials where germs are imagined as short, fat, grumpy old men don't help.

But for their own development, children must explore and try new things even if it means getting dirty or, heaven forbid, skinning a knee. Perhaps a good analogy is that God doesn't coddle *us* to the degree that we coddle our children. God lets us make mistakes, fall down, and skin our proverbial knees. And yet our divine parent is always there to pick us up, dust us off, hug us, and send us on our way. Just as we want our children to succeed in life, God wants us to thrive spiritually. And the way we do so is not by sitting around outside the fray of human contact but by engaging with God in the midst of humanity.

The good news is that there's always bath night to wash away the grime; dirt isn't permanent. For some families, bath time is a calming part of the nightly bedtime ritual. For us it was always a nightmare. "The boys are clean enough, don't you think?" became our mantra. Before we mercifully graduated to showers, the words "bath night" caused fear and trembling in my heart. I think Ben was born hating water being poured on his head, which made his baptism fun. He did just fine playing in the tub—it was the "Okay, it's time to wash hair" that sent him into hysterics. We tried every bath toy in creation to distract him from the dreaded hair washing, but nothing ever worked. I can't imagine what our neighbors thought we were doing to him as he screamed like an extra in *The Texas Chainsaw Massacre*.

Unless you want your kid to grow up to be Mr. Clean—complete with bald head and earring—it's probably best to relax a bit. Sure, germs and dirt are out there. Kids will ruin some clothes and catch a virus along the way. They might even need stitches before they graduate from elementary school. Just pray that it happens on your spouse's watch, not yours.

Mail Call

I like getting the mail. It's a simple pleasure, and while I'm often disappointed in the result, there's something about opening the mailbox each day. On a small scale it feeds that part of me that never outgrew the joy of opening a gift. You never quite know what the mail will bring: a letter from an old friend, an invitation to a party, my copy of *Sports Illustrated*. Usually I get a handful of solicitation letters, catalogs—which Bryna actually "reads"—and bills. But there's always the hope of finding a gem amidst the junk.

I'd never admit to anyone that my heart skips a beat when I spy the mail truck. It's pretty lame to look back on your day and realize that mail call was the highlight. Unless you're serving overseas in the armed forces, there's no excuse for this. Especially because it tends to be the single most anticlimactic moment of my day; there's rarely much in the pile that justifies the sense of expectation.

Nonetheless, I find myself lying in wait for the mail carrier. As the hour of delivery draws near, I start looking out the window. Just a glance every few minutes. My ears perk up when I hear a vehicle approach like a dog listening for the sound of the family van in the driveway. And then, finally, I catch a glimpse of the long-awaited red, white, and blue truck. I don't race out to meet the mail man; I do have a shred of dignity. I don't want him to think I'm a stalker, so I play it cool. I wait until he drives up to the next house and *then* I pounce.

The boys don't seem to have inherited my full-blown mail addiction. Maybe it comes with growing up in the e-mail age. Anyway, there are only two types of letters they get on a regular basis: birthday party invitations and birthday party thank-you notes. They get as many of these as I get credit card bills. But whenever I grab the mail and walk up the driveway at home, the first question is always, "Did I get anything?" The answer is usually "Not today" followed by the advice my parents always gave me when I asked the same question: "You need to send a letter to get a letter." Well, that's annoying.

I also seem to get a lot of publications with donor lists: alumni magazines, annual reports from various nonprofit groups, and church publications. I've always been intrigued when I see the name "anonymous" turn up on these lists. I wonder just what motivates someone to give anonymously. Is it to brag to a few close friends about your wonderful act of selflessness? Is it to feel even better about yourself because you're not seeking public recognition for a good deed? Or are there some people who just genuinely and quietly give from their hearts? I can't recall ever giving money anonymously to a school or a church or any other organization. In fact, I admit that when I get the annual issue of my college alumni magazine that lists all the donors from the past year, I immediately turn to find my name. It better be spelled right, and it had better be listed in the correct financial bracket. Of course, if they mistakenly put me in a higher category, that's fine.

But after I've scrolled down the page and have finally found my name, I can't help but question my own motivation for giving. Have I given because I truly care about the mission of the institution? Have I given because I want to see my name in print? Have I given because I want *others* to see my name in print? Have I given because I want a tax write-off? In reality, it's probably a combination of these. And I find it helpful to reflect upon the question of how my giving would differ if it were all done anonymously. Would I give to the same organizations? Would I give more or less? What exactly is my real motivation for giving?

Ben's Taekwondo instructor talks to the kids a lot about integrity. He defines it as the way you act when no one's looking. If he's not watching the students, do they still try their best? Are the kicks just as crisp and strong when his back is turned as when he's staring at them? If not, they're displaying a lack of integrity.

Maybe it would be helpful if we lived our lives as if we were being watched. Not out of fear, as if a video surveillance camera was pointed in our direction to catch us doing something wrong. But out of an awareness that our motivations and actions in this life do matter. And actually, this isn't so far from the truth. Because the God "to whom all hearts are open, all desires known, and from whom no secrets are hid" (Book of Common Prayer), is watching us. God is not an Orwellian Big Brother type. But God is intimately aware of our inward motivations and outward actions. Which is one reason why God's forgiveness is such a wonderful and valuable gift. Loving grace pours out upon us *despite* what God knows about us and our less-than-pure motivations.

Maybe I'll give anonymously the next time I send a check to my seminary. Then when the alumni magazine comes, I can pretend I was that anonymous donor in the $15,000 to $20,000 range. Oh, wait, that misses the point. Well, consider giving anonymously the next time you make a donation to a church. And I'll try not to be too aggravated that there's no mail delivery on Sundays.

Listen Up!

Like many of my fellow men, I have an uncanny ability to listen without really hearing. I'm not sure if this is an innate gift, honed over thousands of years to an art form, or whether it's a learned trait. But I can hold down conversations on a wide variety of topics, inserting the appropriate grunts of affirmation and acknowledgment, while simultaneously reading the sports section of *The New York Times*. It's quite amazing actually. At least until I invariably foul it up by asking Bryna what she's doing tomorrow after she mentioned her plans just moments before. And, once again, I get caught red-handed listening but not really hearing.

You might even call it selective listening. If there was a topic of great interest to me, I would probably hear it. If not, it ends up being filtered out. Good gossip comes straight through, but discussing what colors we're going to paint the dining room tends to fade into the background.

The boys do the same thing to me, so I'm starting to have more sympathy for Bryna's plight as the only female in the house. Besides Delilah. I guess all kids do this to annoy their parents. But when I'm staring at Ben telling him to pick up his stuffed animals that are strewn across the family room like there's been a jailbreak at the Bronx Zoo and it doesn't register, it makes me crazy. He sits there immobilized like a marble statue at the Louvre, except with arms. I'd like to know what's going through his head. Is there silence? Does he hear me but is just ignoring me? Do I sound like the parents on Charlie Brown making those unintelligible honking sounds? It's hard to tell because nothing seems to register. As with me, certain things break through the barrier. If I asked him if he'd like to take a quick trip to Carvel, he'd be out the door and buckled into the minivan before I could find my keys. But asking him to pick up his baseball cards creates an impenetrable force field of deafness. At least for the first five times I ask him the same question.

Bryna's always quick to point out that my phrasing in addressing the boys is flawed. There's a difference between her "Ben, put your Batman costume away" and my "Ben, do you mind picking that costume up?" "Never in the form of a question," she hisses at me. And she's right—it's one of those Parenting 101 basics I regularly seem to forget. But I don't think it matters much when they're in the nonhearing "zone."

One of the most ancient and well-beloved passages of Scripture is known as the Great Shema: "Hear, O Israel: The Lord is our God, the Lord alone. You shall love the Lord your God with all your heart, and with all your soul, and with all your might" (Deuteronomy 6:4–5). Shema comes from the Hebrew word "hear" and is pronounced *shə-mah'*. It's not the Great Shamu, as I once heard someone call it. You'll find that at Sea World. But it's interesting that this is such an important passage in the Judeo-Christian tradition because it implies that we need reminders to pay attention to God. It's so easy to hear the voice of God but not really listen to it.

Let's face it, we're forgetful creatures. So we write out to-do lists, we set alarms, we tie strings around our fingers. But perhaps the best reminders of all are those yellow sticky things, technically known as Post-it notes. I'm not sure how society survived before they were created. Certainly no church could have unless people were just accustomed to clergy losing their place during services. I'm a big fan of Post-it notes. They always seem to be in abundance, and they're hard to miss. That yellow color stands out amid the clutter of most desks or kitchens, which is precisely the point. If you stick one on your computer or on your phone, there's no way you won't see it. They are great reminders. Though I admit I'm a traditionalist when it comes to these things—they've got to be yellow. Orange, green, or, God forbid, purple Post-it notes should all be sent through the shredder.

When I was newly ordained and serving my first church in Baltimore, I put a Post-it note on my computer at the office. It held a daily reminder to me about the point of my ministry and my preaching. On it I had written, "It's the Gospel, stupid"—a variation on James Carville's famous attempt to keep the 1992 Clinton presidential campaign "on message." For me the note served as a helpful reminder to keep me focused on the task at hand. We all need those reminders, and God knows our forgetful ways. If we would only remember God, not only with our lips but in our lives, God wouldn't have to keep reminding us. But we are a forgetful people, forgetful of the one who creates and redeems us. And forgetfulness leads us onto that slippery slope toward apathy, that self-delusional state where we believe that we can get by without God's help. Which we cannot. And it's why we need that constant reminder from God to "hear" so that we can cross that boundary from listening to hearing. Something I desperately need to work on at home. But at least, with the boys around, I'm in good company.

Free Fall

I'm afraid of heights. Or at least I don't enjoy them very much. Sure, I've been to the observation deck of the Empire State Building and I've been dragged to the top of the Gateway Arch in St. Louis. But you won't catch me bungee jumping or cliff diving. It's just not my thing.

So it was slightly out of character when, as a young Army ROTC cadet, I got the idea that I wanted to become a paratrooper. They're the ones that jump out of airplanes (yes, while in flight). Maybe it was peer pressure—most of my friends were airborne qualified. Maybe it was the desire to face my fears. Most likely it was temporary insanity. But whatever the reason, I found myself at Fort Benning that August doing thousands of push-ups in the sweltering Georgia heat as I trained to make the required five jumps to earn my airborne wings.

After two weeks of ground training, and plenty of verbal "encouragement" from the instructors, it was time to jump for real. Although I had received some of the army's best training, once I boarded that C-130 for my first jump I was left to confront my own fears, doubts, and anxieties. All sorts of questions swirled in my head as that beast of a plane roared down the runway. Will my parachute actually work? Have I seen my family and friends for the last time? And, as people tend to get quite religious in such situations, will God help me get through this?

Believe it or not, the army even provided an airborne chaplain to jump with us. I wasn't sure if he was there to offer comfort or Last Rites. Uncle Sam also issued all of us budding paratroopers "barf bags" before we boarded the plane. The only stipulation being that if you used it, you had to take it with you when you jumped.

As I sat in the airplane waiting to jump for the first time, my eyes kept focusing on the open door. As the light above it changed from red to green indicating that we were over the drop zone, my heart pounded. The noise from the engines was deafening, and I looked around to try and get a glimpse of that chaplain. I shuffled toward the door with eighty pounds of parachute and equipment strapped tightly to my body. The jumpmaster yelled "Go!" and I flung myself out the door.

Leaping out into the unknown is an apt metaphor for parenting. You do the research, you read the books, you take Lamaze classes, and attend parenting seminars, although there is *no* correlation between changing a doll's diaper and that of a squirmy, shrieking infant who just peed all over you. But until you experience the miracle of creation firsthand, the idea remains an abstraction. First-time parenting certainly brings new meaning to the phrase "on-the-job training."

After Bryna and I brought Ben home from the maternity ward of Evanston Hospital, we just stared at him for a while, waiting for the "real" parents to show up. This helpless newborn sitting in a car seat didn't even come with an instruction manual. But, as with jumping out of an airplane for the first time, you have no choice but to confront your fears and start parenting. You make some mistakes, you get frustrated, but you just keep loving them as best you can and you trust that God will take care of the rest.

Making it back to earth in one piece after that first jump was exhilarating. It was also decidedly not a soft landing. The army doesn't use those big square parachutes you see at demonstrations where jumpers land standing up. The point of a military jump is, of course, to get as many people on the ground in as short a time as possible. So landing is equivalent to jumping off a ten-foot wall. Which is why you spend one whole week out of three at airborne school learning how to fall. I'll never like heights, but it's nice to know that I can deal with them if I have to. I'm just never going on the Cyclone at Coney Island.

It is my sincere hope that these stories have offered some encouragement and inspiration along your own journey of joy and chaos. When you're up at 3:00 a.m. with a sick kid deciding whether or not to head out to the ER and you're simultaneously stressed out and exhausted from a family situation or an issue at work, life feels like a free fall. It's here where an active faith becomes critical. It may not immediately solve everything, but at least you're able to recognize there's an open parachute above you to slow your fall. You can endure anything, even if your landing is a bit bumpy. And that's comforting. God is in the midst of it all even when life itself feels like that proverbial leap of faith.